DATE DUE

NOV 2 6 2019			

DEMCO 38-296

TAKE IT AS A COMPLIMENT.

NAPERVILLE NORTH HIGH SCHOOL
99 NORTH MILL STREET
NAPERVILLE, IL 60563-8998

CONTENTS

ONE

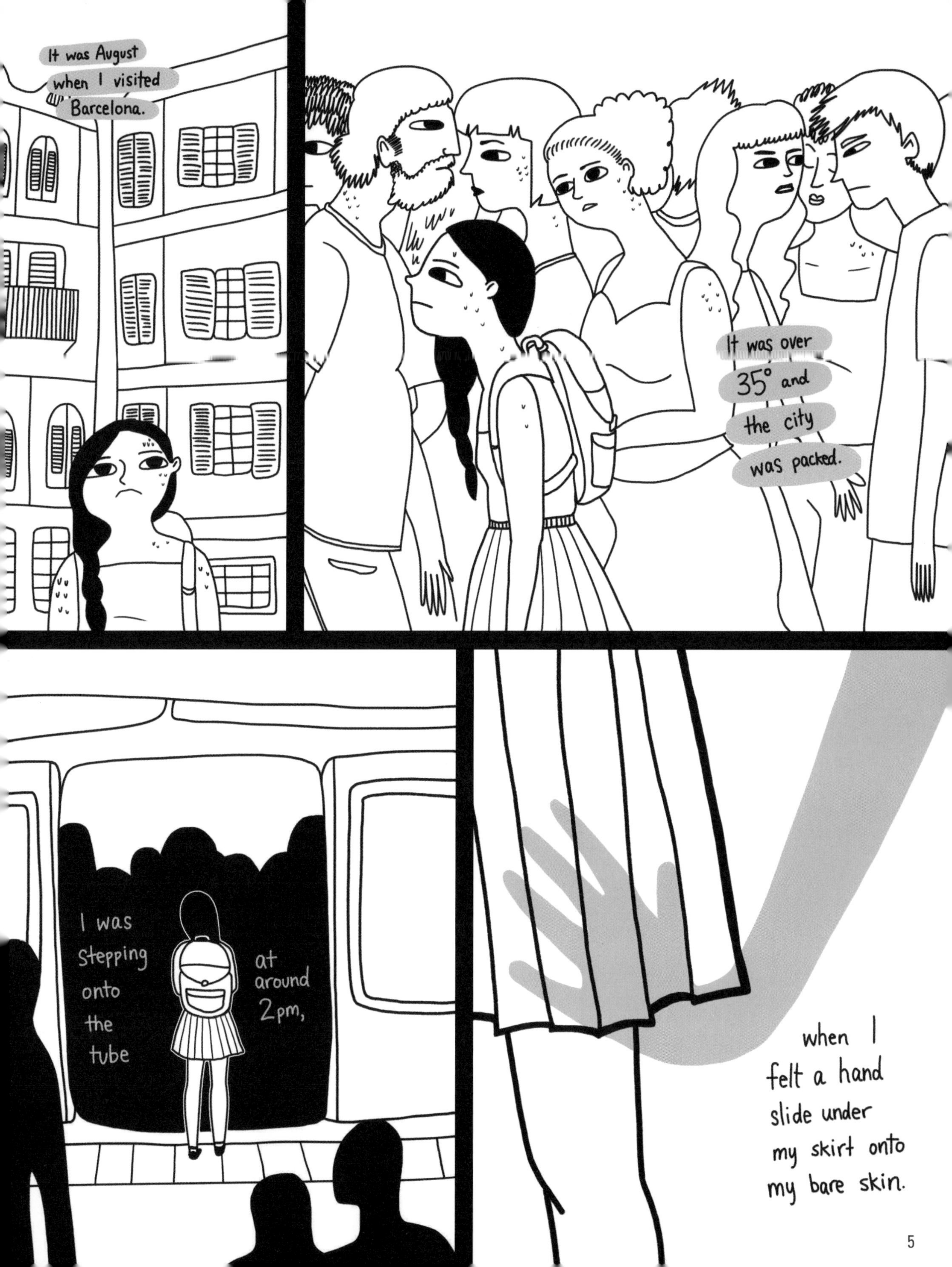
It was August
when I visited
Barcelona.
It was over
35° and
the city
was packed.
I was stepping onto the tube
at around 2pm,
when I felt a hand slide under my skirt onto my bare skin.

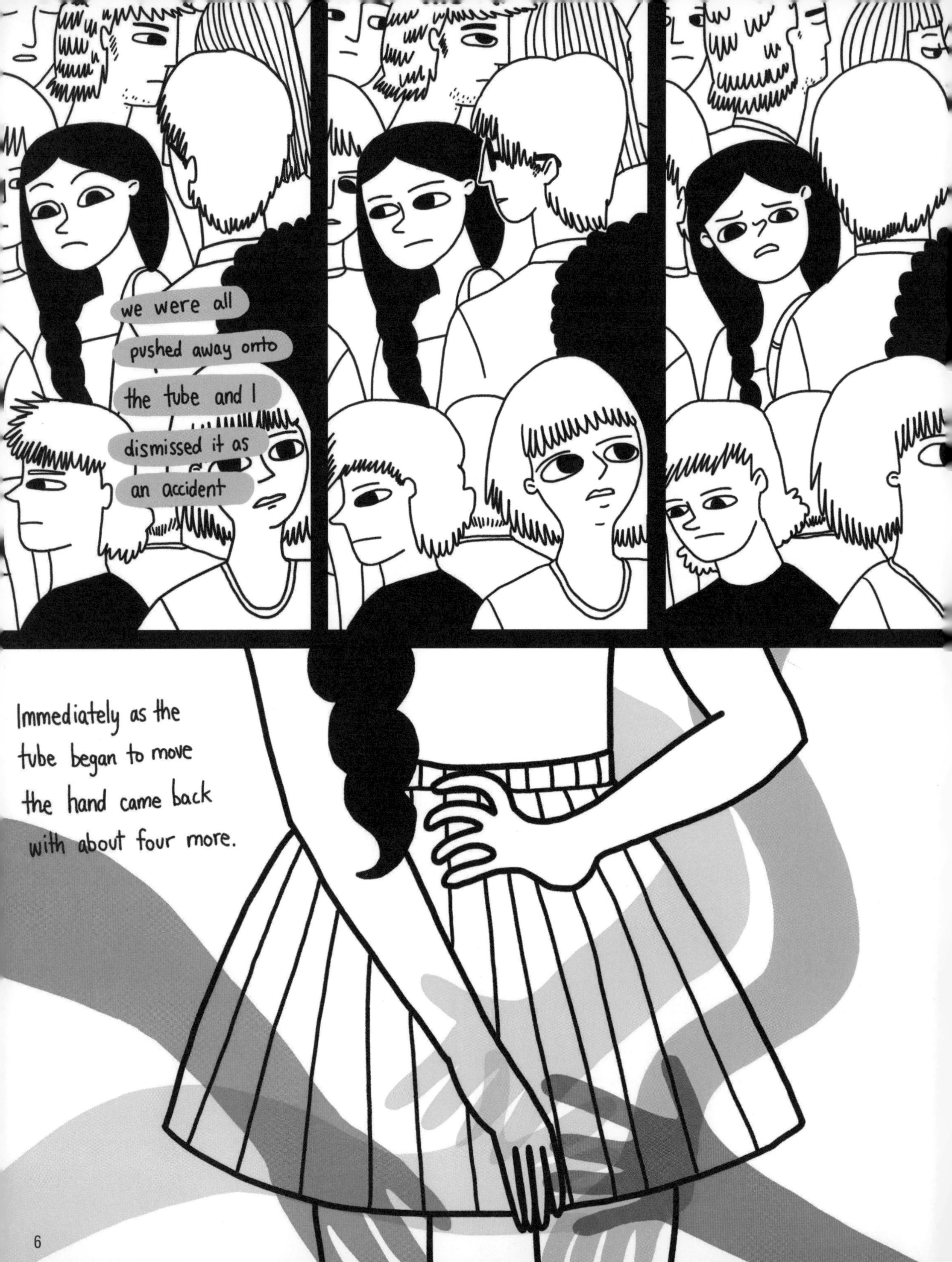
we were all
pushed away onto
the tube and I
dismissed it as
an accident
Immediately as the tube began to move the hand came back with about four more.

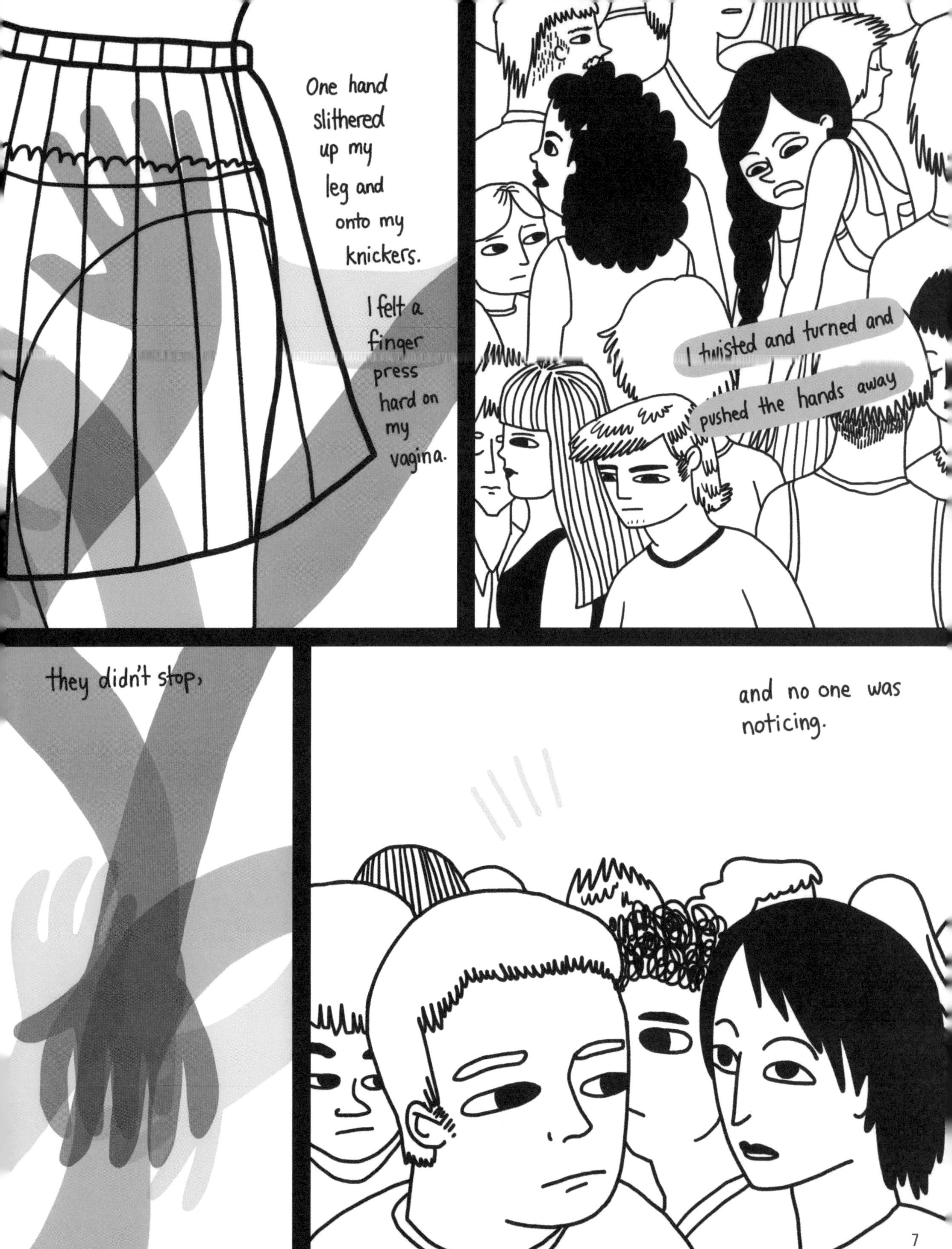
One hand slithered up my leg and onto my knickers.
I felt a finger press hard on my vagina.
I twisted and turned and pushed the hands away
they didn't stop,
and no one was noticing.

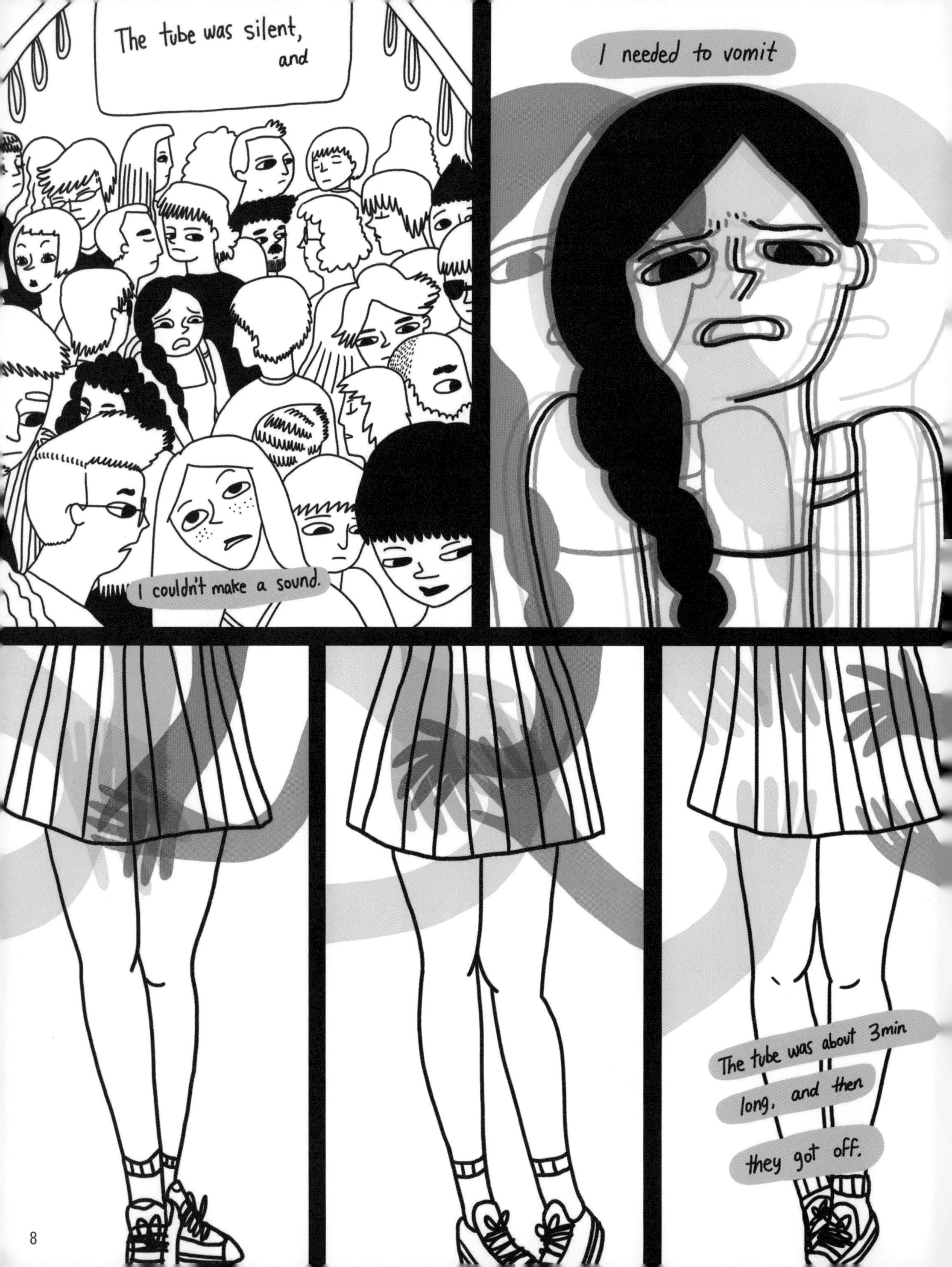
The tube was silent,
and
I couldn't make a sound.
I needed to vomit
The tube was about 3min
long, and then
they got off.

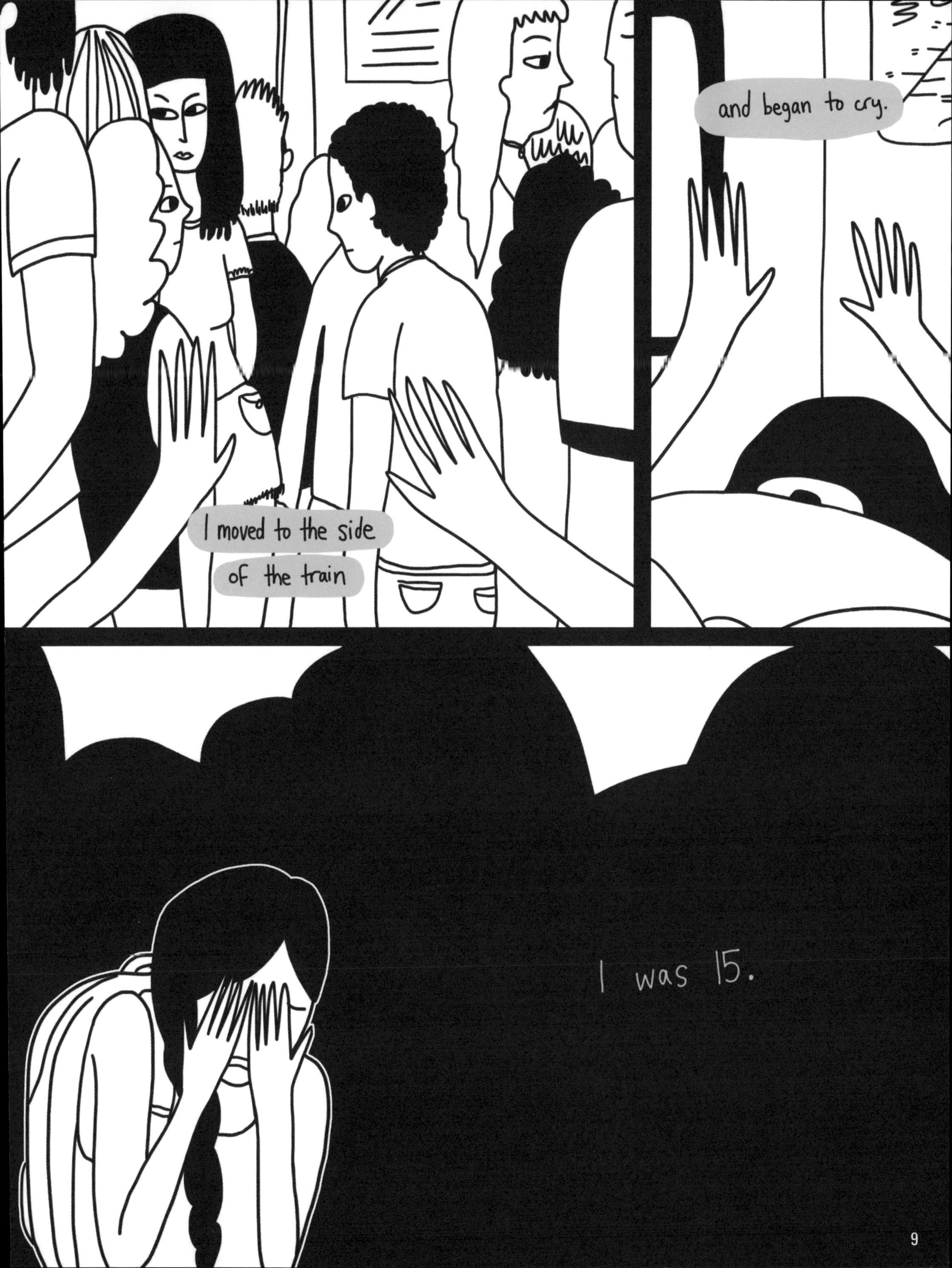
I moved to the side
of the train
and began to cry.
I was 15.

TWO

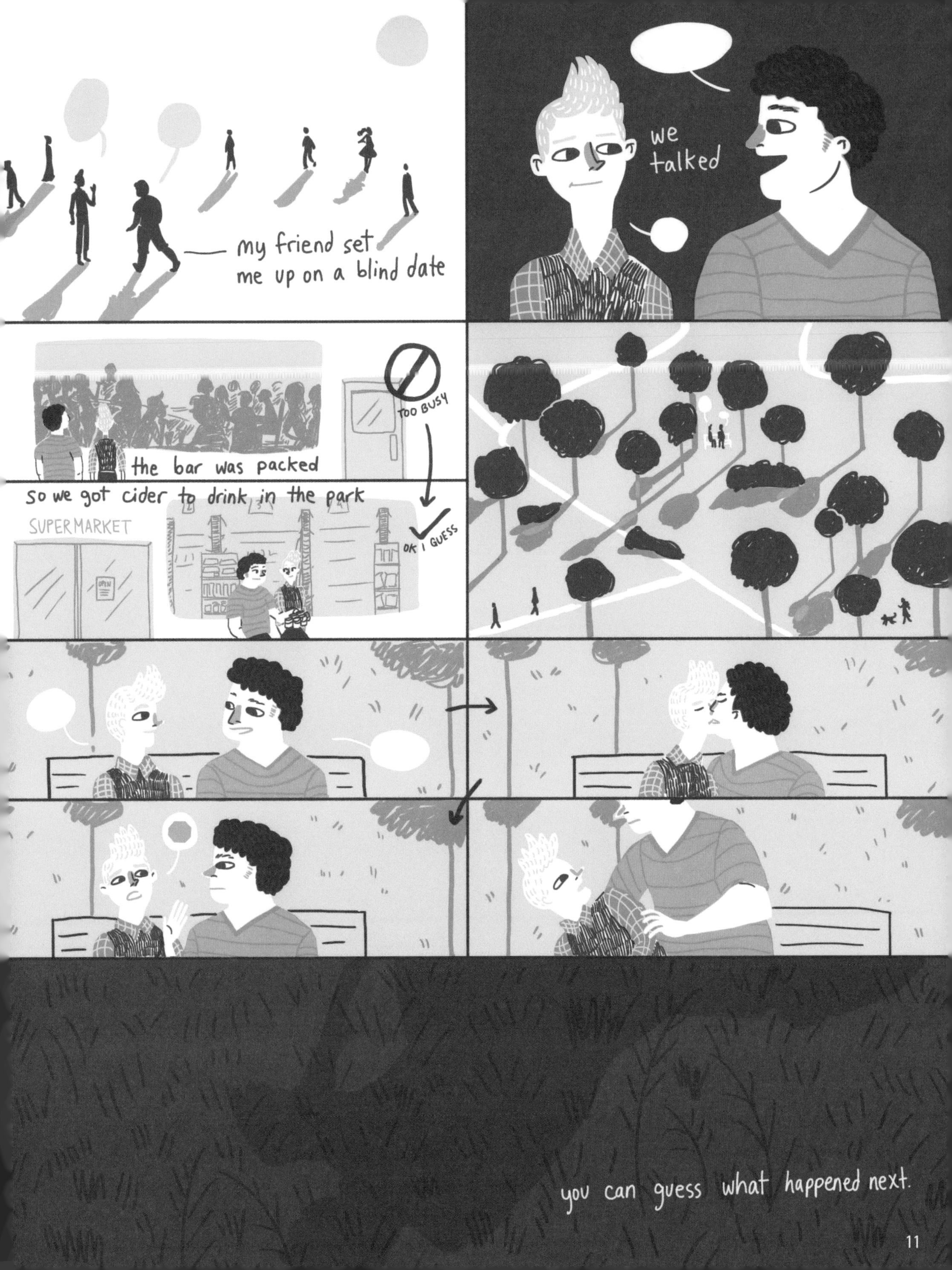
my friend set me up on a blind date
we talked
the bar was packed
TOO BUSY
so we got cider to drink in the park
SUPERMARKET
OK I GUESS
you can guess what happened next.

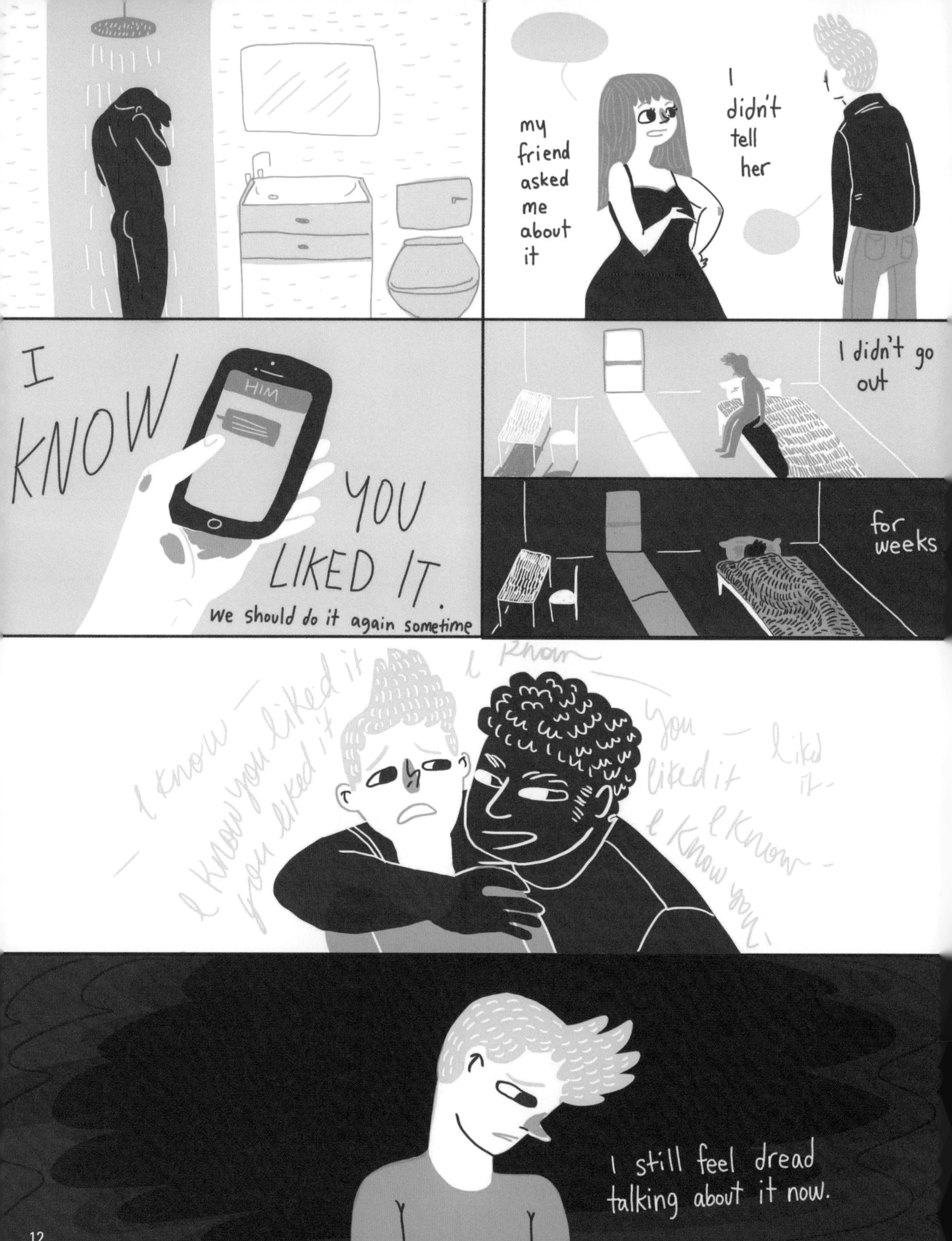
my friend asked me about it
I didn't tell her
I KNOW YOU LIKED IT.
HIM
we should do it again sometime
I didn't go out
for weeks
I know
I know you liked it
you liked it
you
liked it
liked it
I know
I know you
I still feel dread talking about it now.

THREE

my first real relationship

turned out to be abusive.

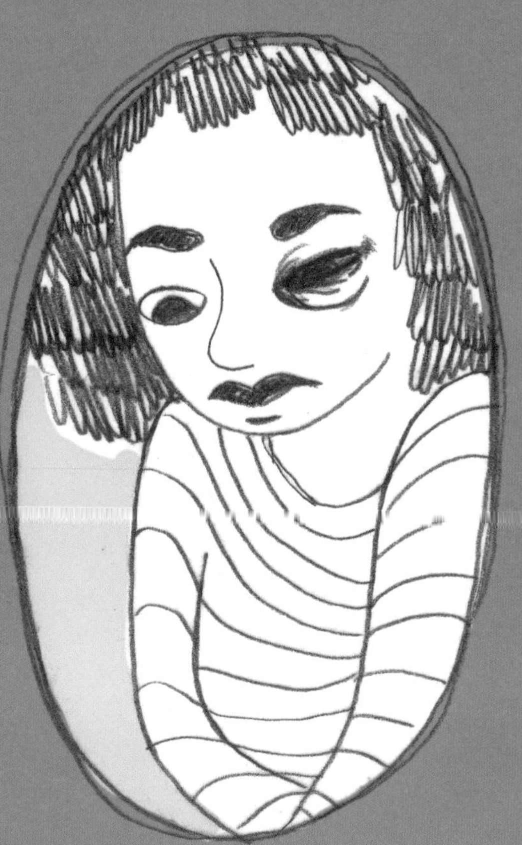

physically,

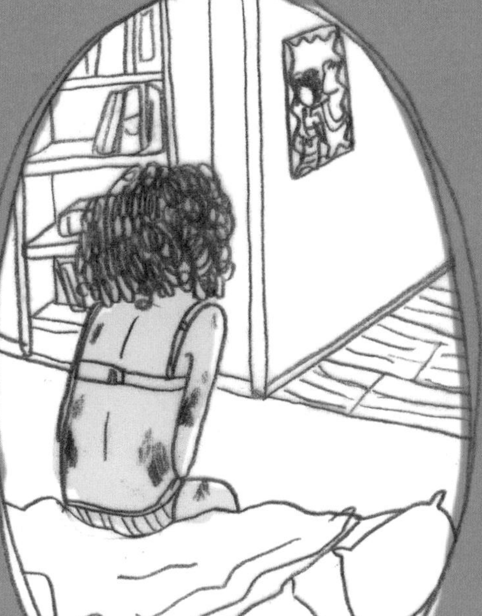

sexually,

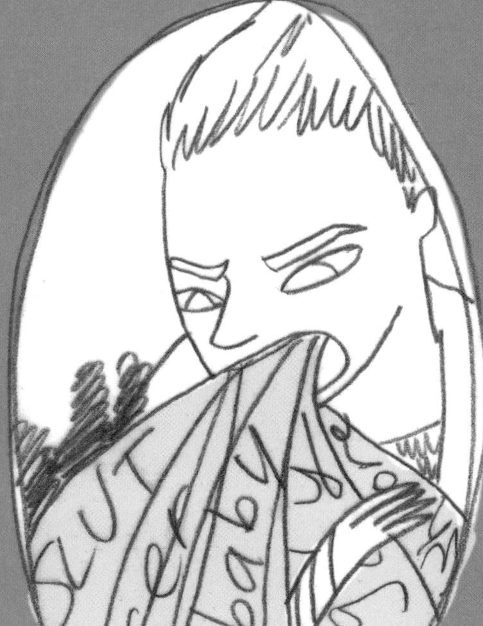
SLUT
loser
crybaby

and verbally.

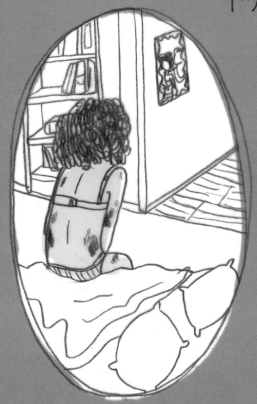

I confided in my best friend who was much older than me

and provided great counselling and support.

In the summer I turned 18,
half a year after the end
of the abusive relationship,

I was supposed to go to the
fireworks with said friend,

but we went to eat
in my place first.

that's where the abuse happened.

the feelings of betrayal, guilt, and self-hate cannot be expressed in existing words.

FOUR

Of all the times I've ended up in regrettable sexual situations, the one that will follow me the longest will be the one I remember the least.

The last thing I remember is sitting on a girlfriend's bed drinking cream soda and vodka.

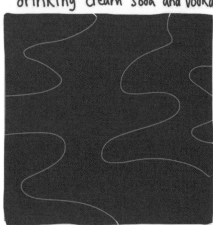

another girl was microwaving pizza pops.

The next thing I remember is waking up in a dark bedroom with a guy I'd barely spoken to. I won't tell you what he was doing, suffice it to say I'll never do it again.

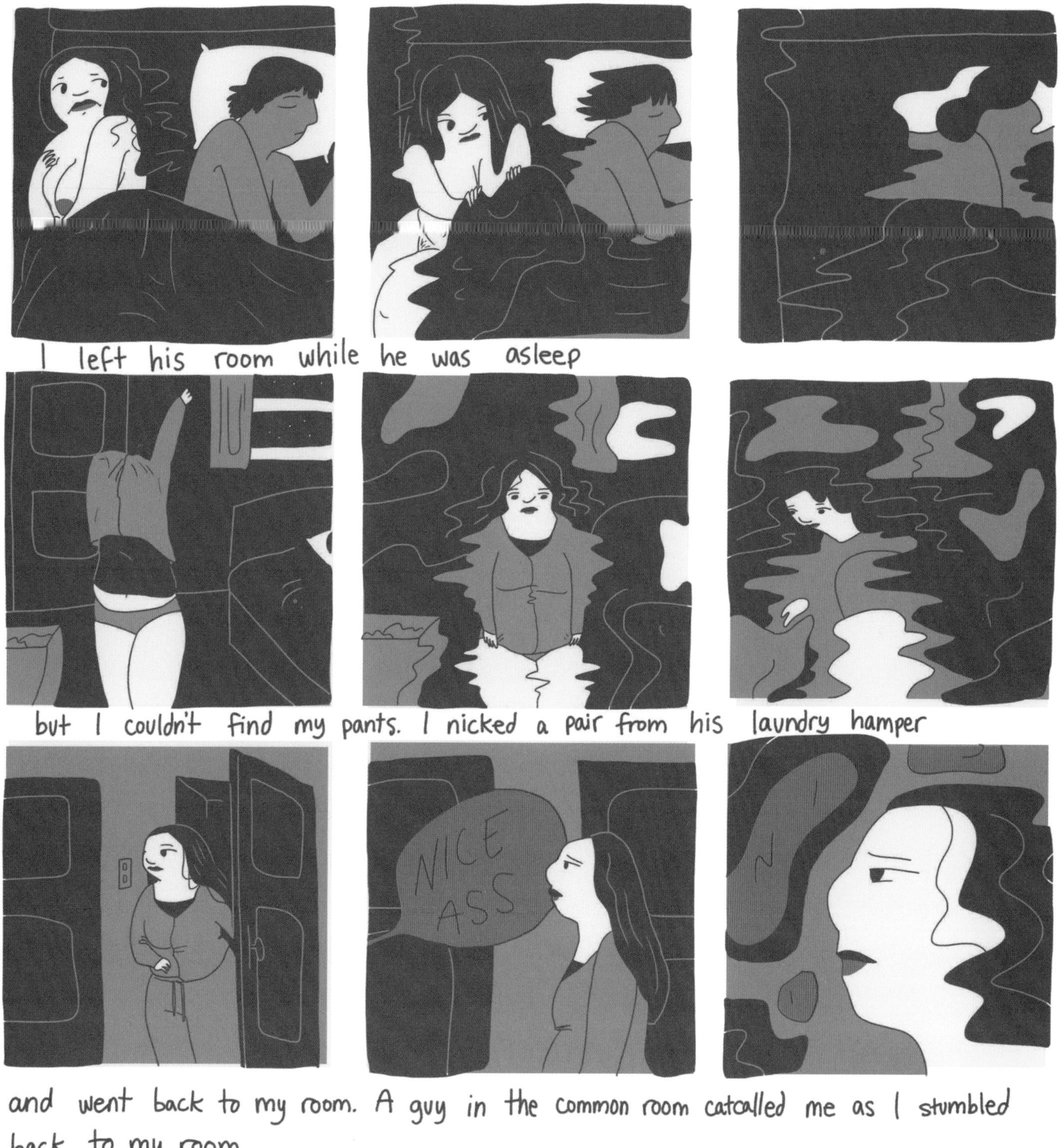
I left his room while he was asleep
but I couldn't find my pants. I nicked a pair from his laundry hamper
NICE ASS
and went back to my room. A guy in the common room catcalled me as I stumbled back to my room.

I woke up the next morning and laundered his sweatpants——

there was blood on them——

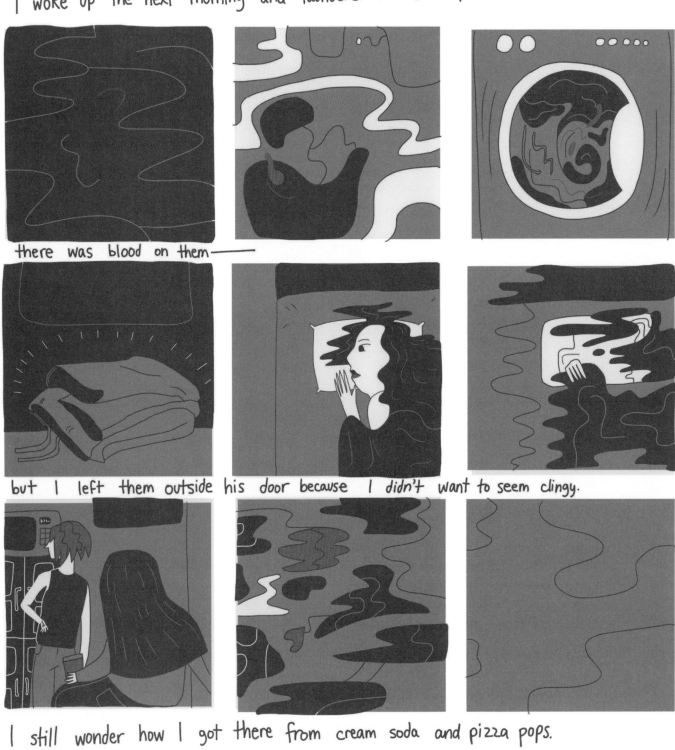

but I left them outside his door because I didn't want to seem clingy.

I still wonder how I got there from cream soda and pizza pops.

FIVE

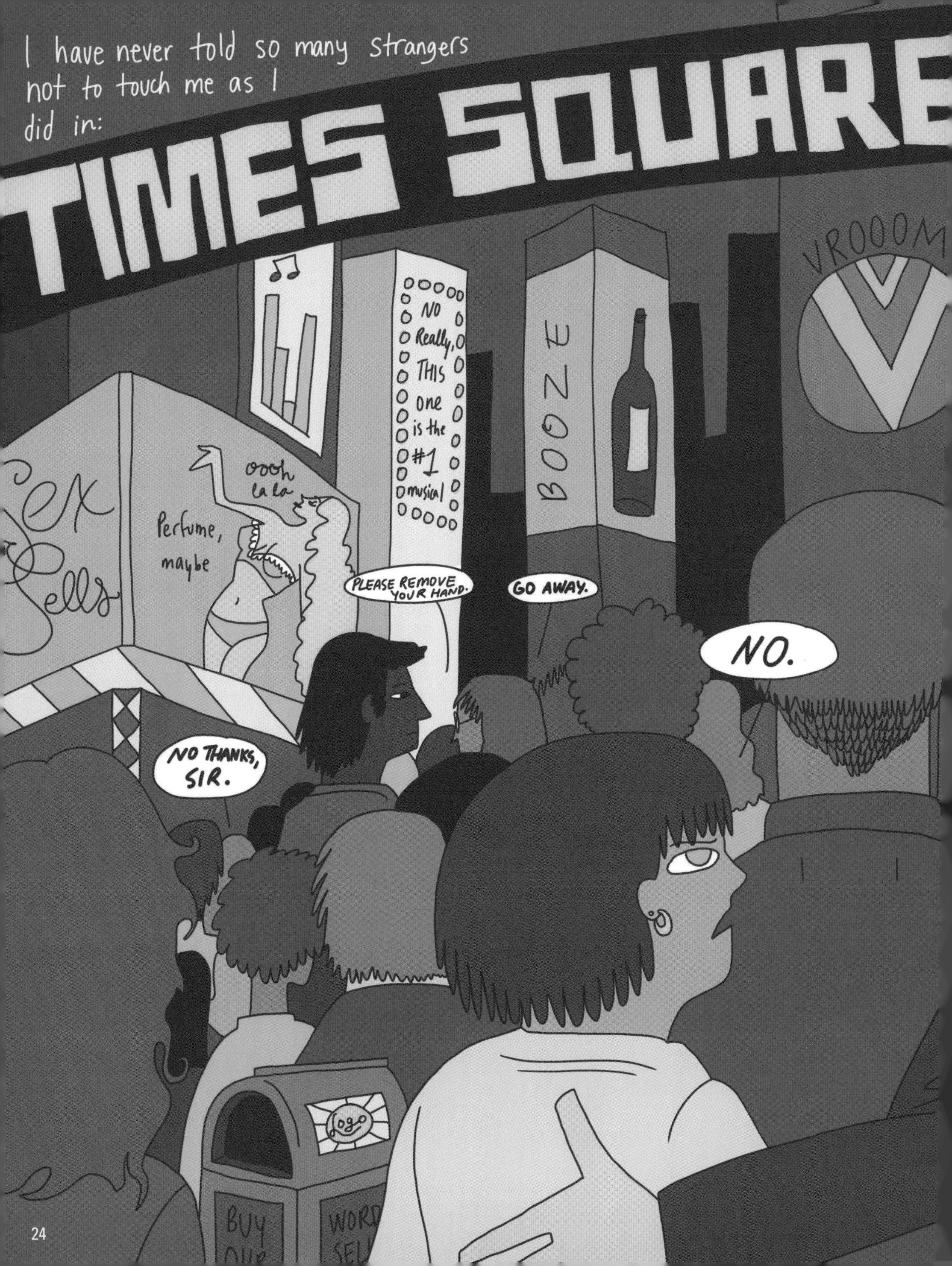
I have never told so many strangers not to touch me as I did in:
TIMES SQUARE
VROOOM
NO Really, THIS one is the #1 musical
BOOZE
Sex Sells
oooh la la
Perfume, maybe
PLEASE REMOVE YOUR HAND.
GO AWAY.
NO.
NO THANKS, SIR.
Logo
BUY
WORD

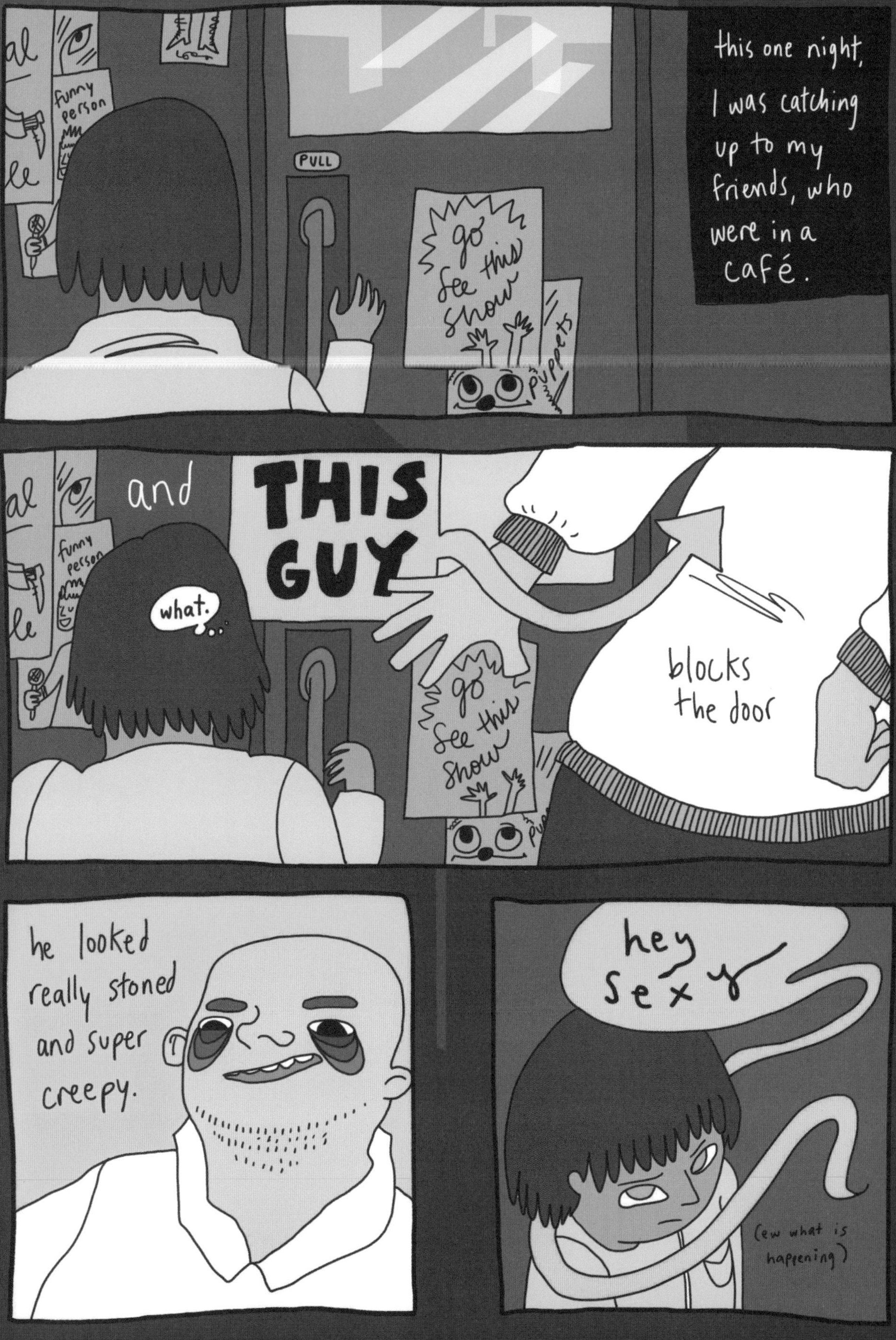
this one night, I was catching up to my friends, who were in a café.
funny person
PULL
go see this show
puppets
and THIS GUY
what.
blocks the door
he looked really stoned and super creepy.
hey sexy
(ew what is happening)

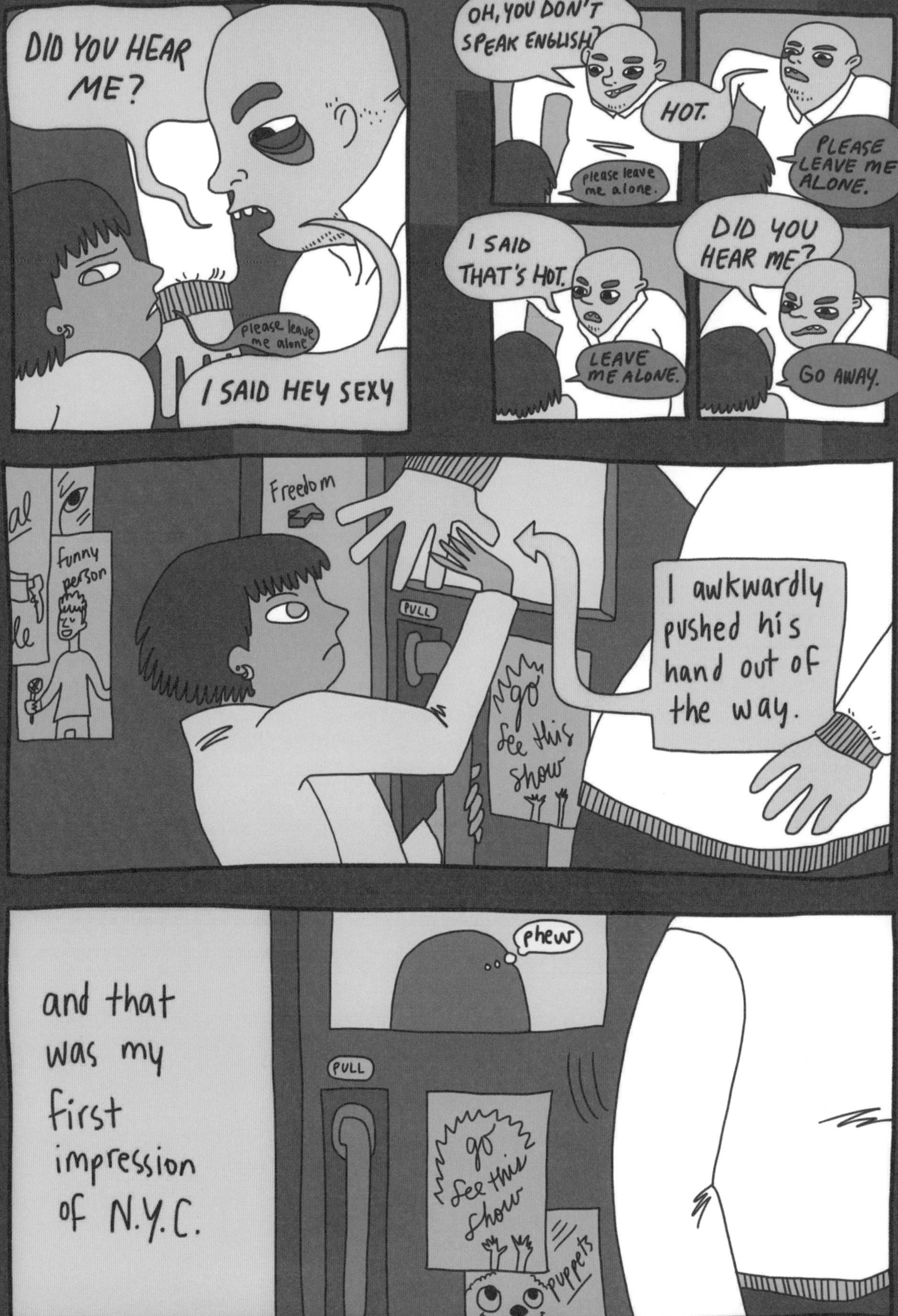

DID YOU HEAR ME?
please leave me alone
I SAID HEY SEXY
OH, YOU DON'T SPEAK ENGLISH?
HOT.
please leave me alone.
PLEASE LEAVE ME ALONE.
I SAID THAT'S HOT.
LEAVE ME ALONE.
DID YOU HEAR ME?
GO AWAY.
Freedom
funny person
PULL
go see this show
I awkwardly pushed his hand out of the way.
and that was my first impression of N.Y.C.
phew
PULL
go see this show
puppets

SIX

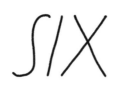

AT THE BUS STOP

HEY, DO YOU GIVE
GOOD HEAD?

MY _BOYFRIEND_
THINKS SO.

SO ARE WE DOING
THIS OR NOT, I
HAVE WORK IN
THE MORNING.

SEVEN

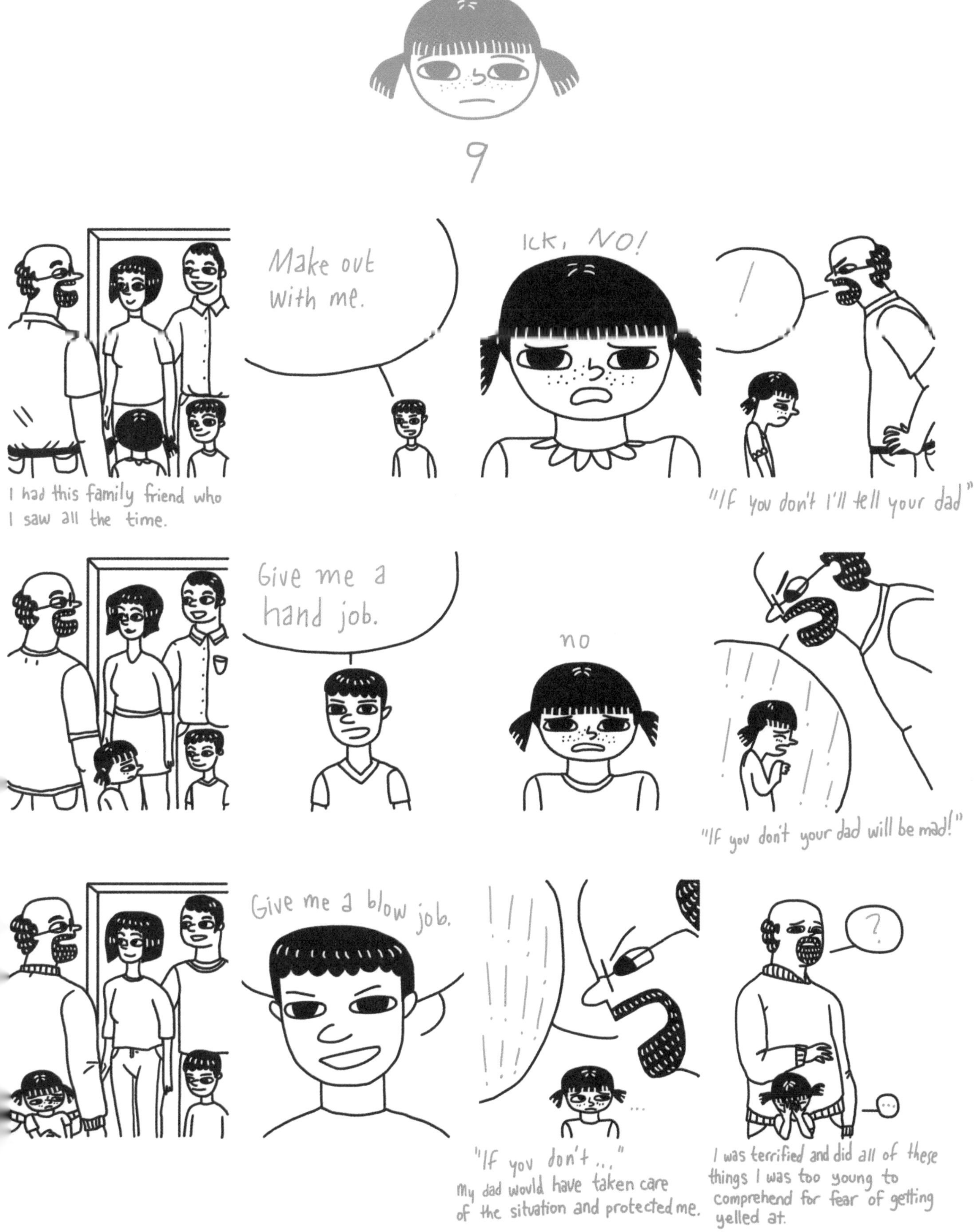
9
I had this family friend who I saw all the time.
Make out with me.
Ick, NO!
!
"If you don't I'll tell your dad"
Give me a hand job.
no
"If you don't your dad will be mad!"
Give me a blow job.
...
"If you don't..."
My dad would have taken care of the situation and protected me.
?
...
I was terrified and did all of these things I was too young to comprehend for fear of getting yelled at.

12

I was over at a friend's house. I had quite the crush on him, but I had a "boyfriend" at the time.

He decided to use my crush to his advantage. I started feeling uncomfortable.

* "I have to go."

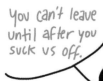

You can't leave until after you suck us off.

"If you don't, I'll tell everyone at school you did."

"Your boyfriend will find out."

"You'll be a joke."

So?

So I did it.

His buddy tried to comfort me afterwards

see ya!

but my "friend" just fucked off.

I haven't really heard from either of them since.

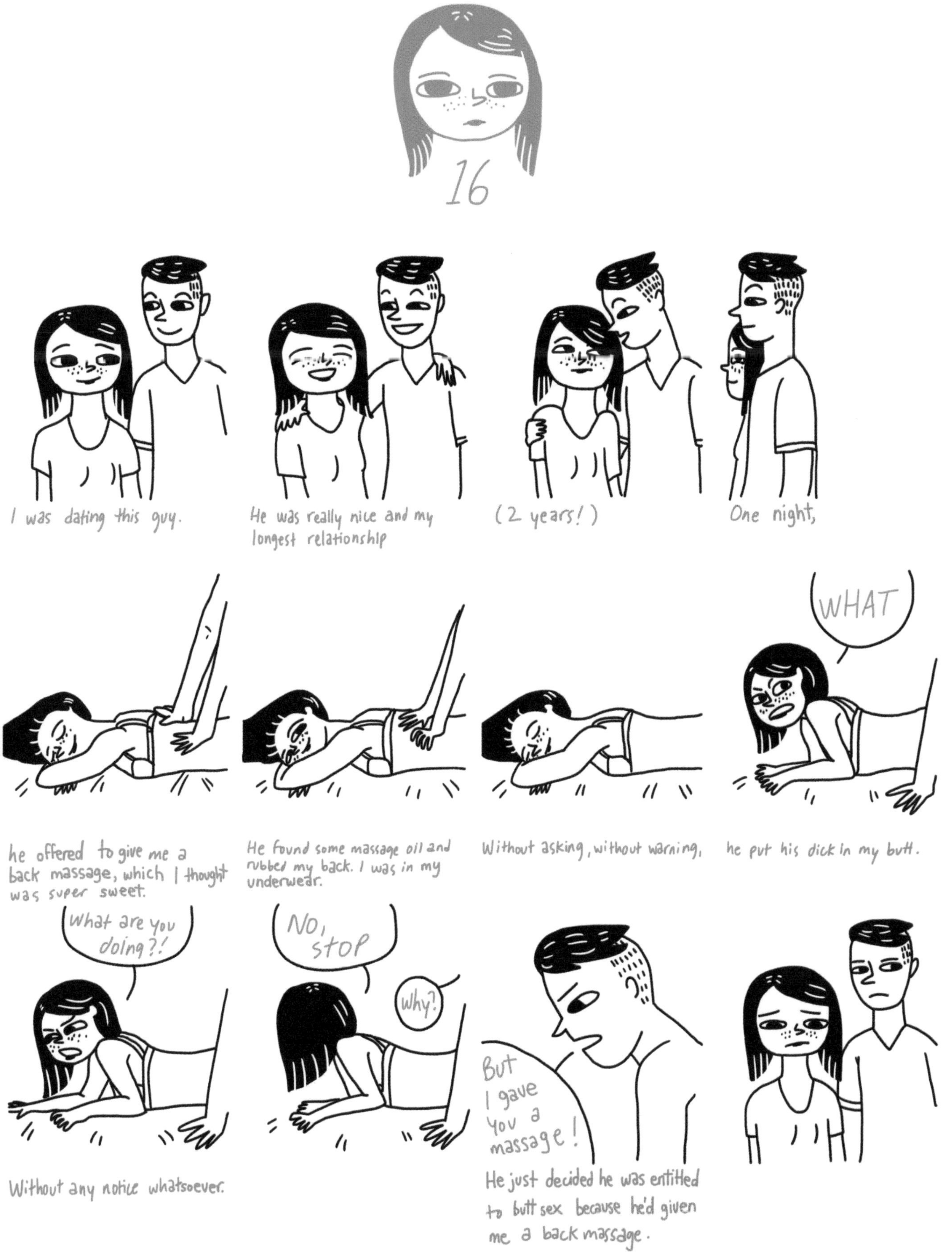
16
I was dating this guy.
He was really nice and my longest relationship
(2 years!)
One night,
he offered to give me a back massage, which I thought was super sweet.
He found some massage oil and rubbed my back. I was in my underwear.
Without asking, without warning,
WHAT
he put his dick in my butt.
What are you doing?!
Without any notice whatsoever.
NO, STOP
Why?
But I gave you a massage!
He just decided he was entitled to butt sex because he'd given me a back massage.

EIGHT

Usually when I tell this story, I say it like it's a funny story. It's easier that way.
I tell it as a story about miscommunication.
B
SPAIN
YOU ARE HERE
A
BERLIN
FRANCE
Of course hitch hiking is all about putting your trust in strangers.
We couldn't really communicate verbally,
<FRENCH>
<PATCHY GERMAN-Y FRENCH>
So we spoke in gestures
MARSEILLES
It would have been a practical arrangement.

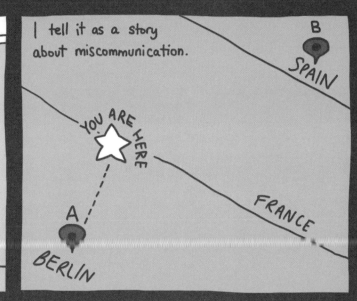

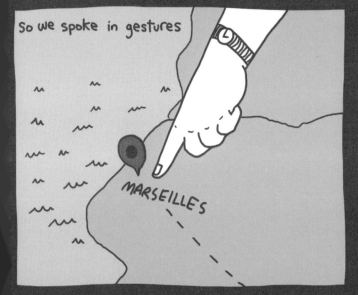

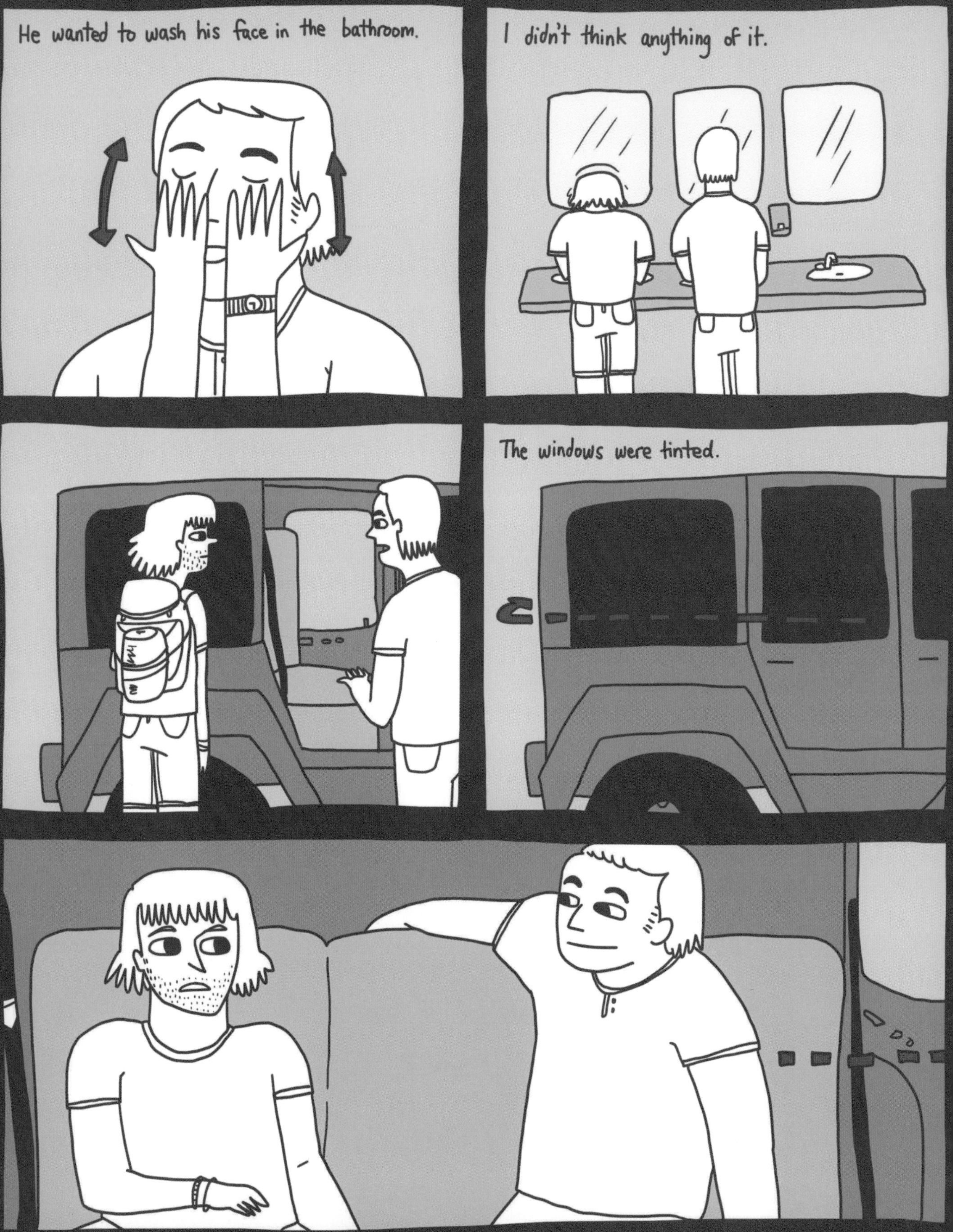
He wanted to wash his face in the bathroom.
I didn't think anything of it.
The windows were tinted.

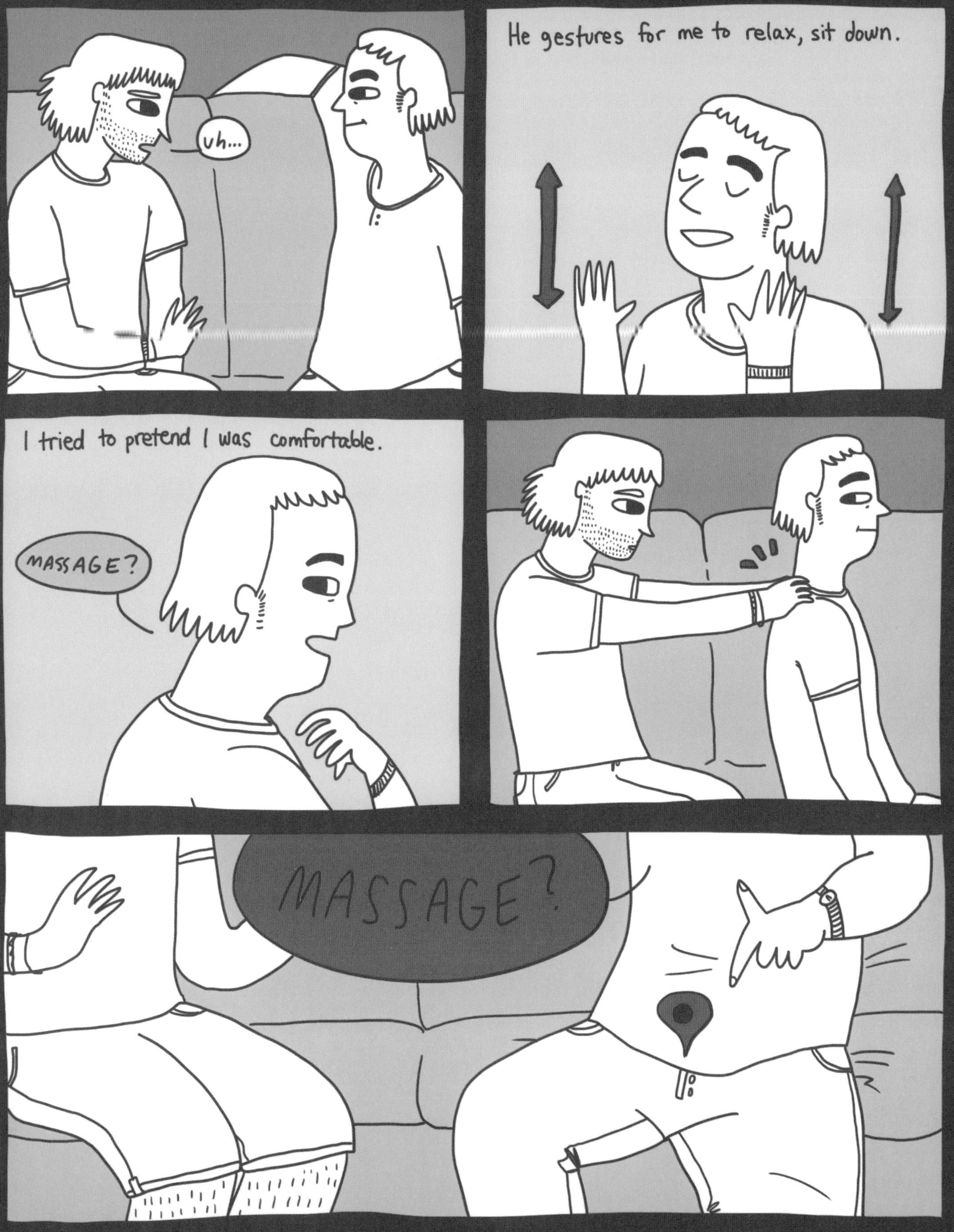
uh...
He gestures for me to relax, sit down.
I tried to pretend I was comfortable.
MASSAGE?
MASSAGE?

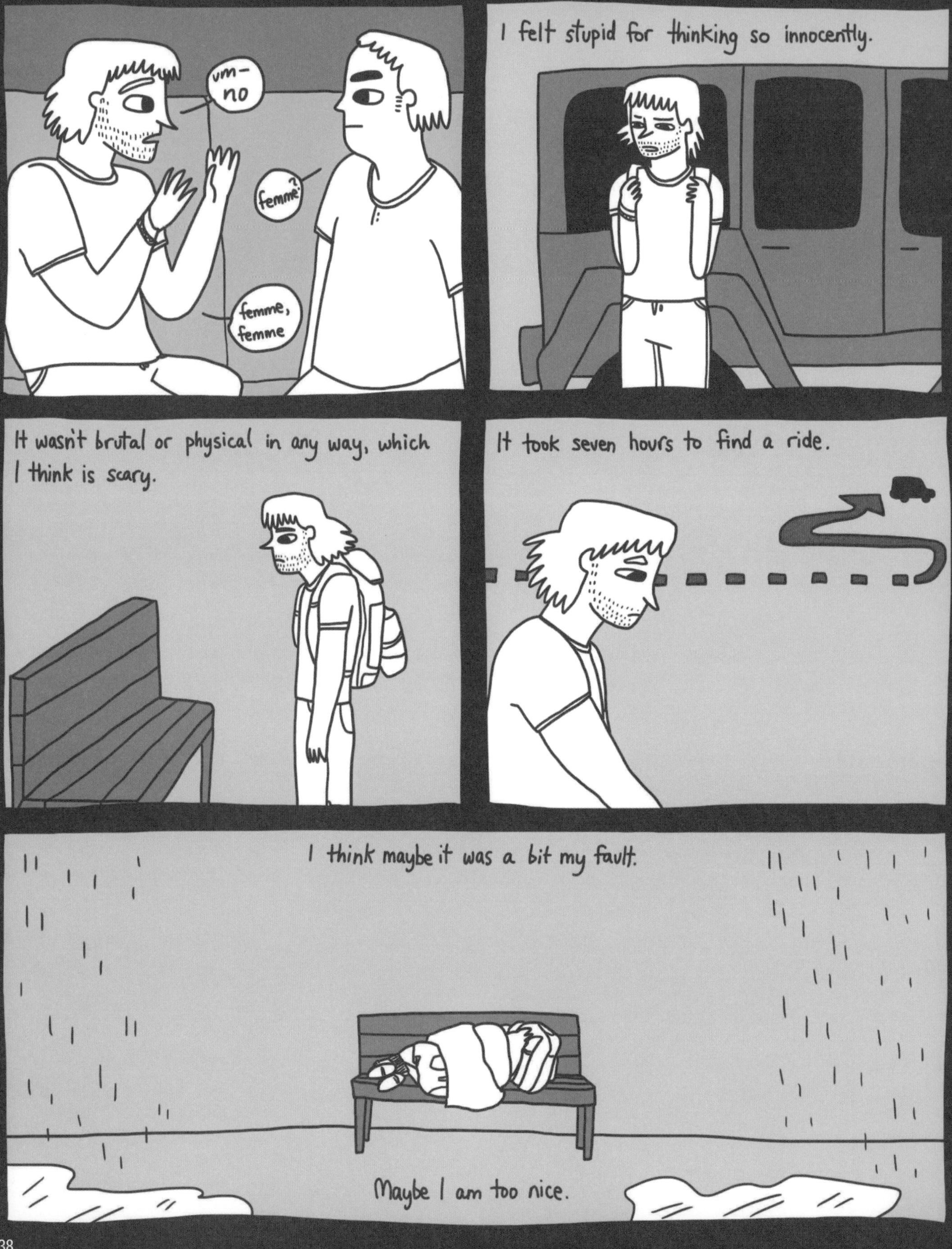
um-
no
femme?
femme,
femme
I felt stupid for thinking so innocently.
It wasn't brutal or physical in any way, which I think is scary.
It took seven hours to find a ride.
I think maybe it was a bit my fault.
Maybe I am too nice.

NINE

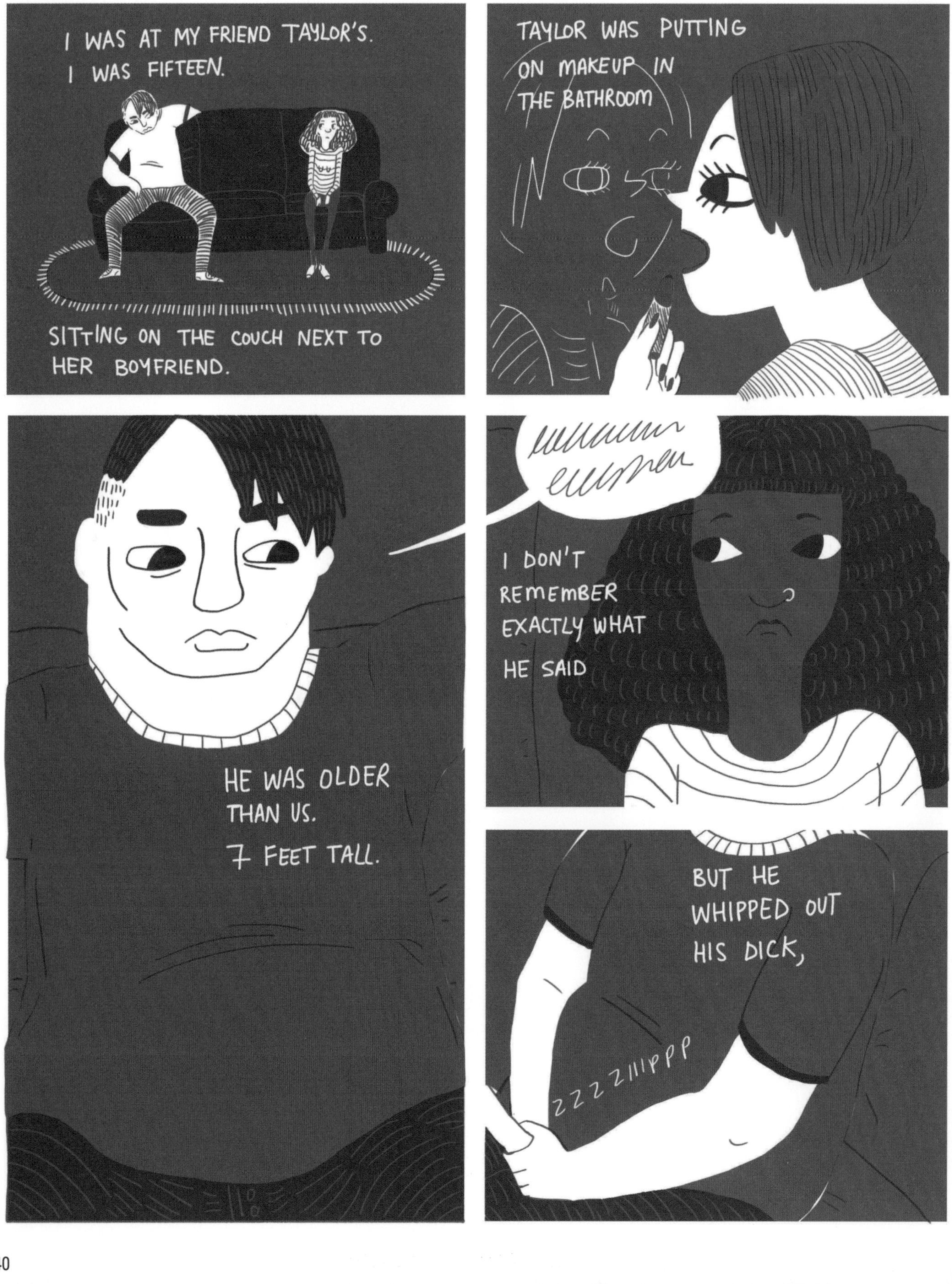
I WAS AT MY FRIEND TAYLOR'S.
I WAS FIFTEEN.
SITTING ON THE COUCH NEXT TO HER BOYFRIEND.
TAYLOR WAS PUTTING ON MAKEUP IN THE BATHROOM
HE WAS OLDER THAN US.
7 FEET TALL.
I DON'T REMEMBER EXACTLY WHAT HE SAID
BUT HE WHIPPED OUT HIS DICK,
ZZZZIIIPPP

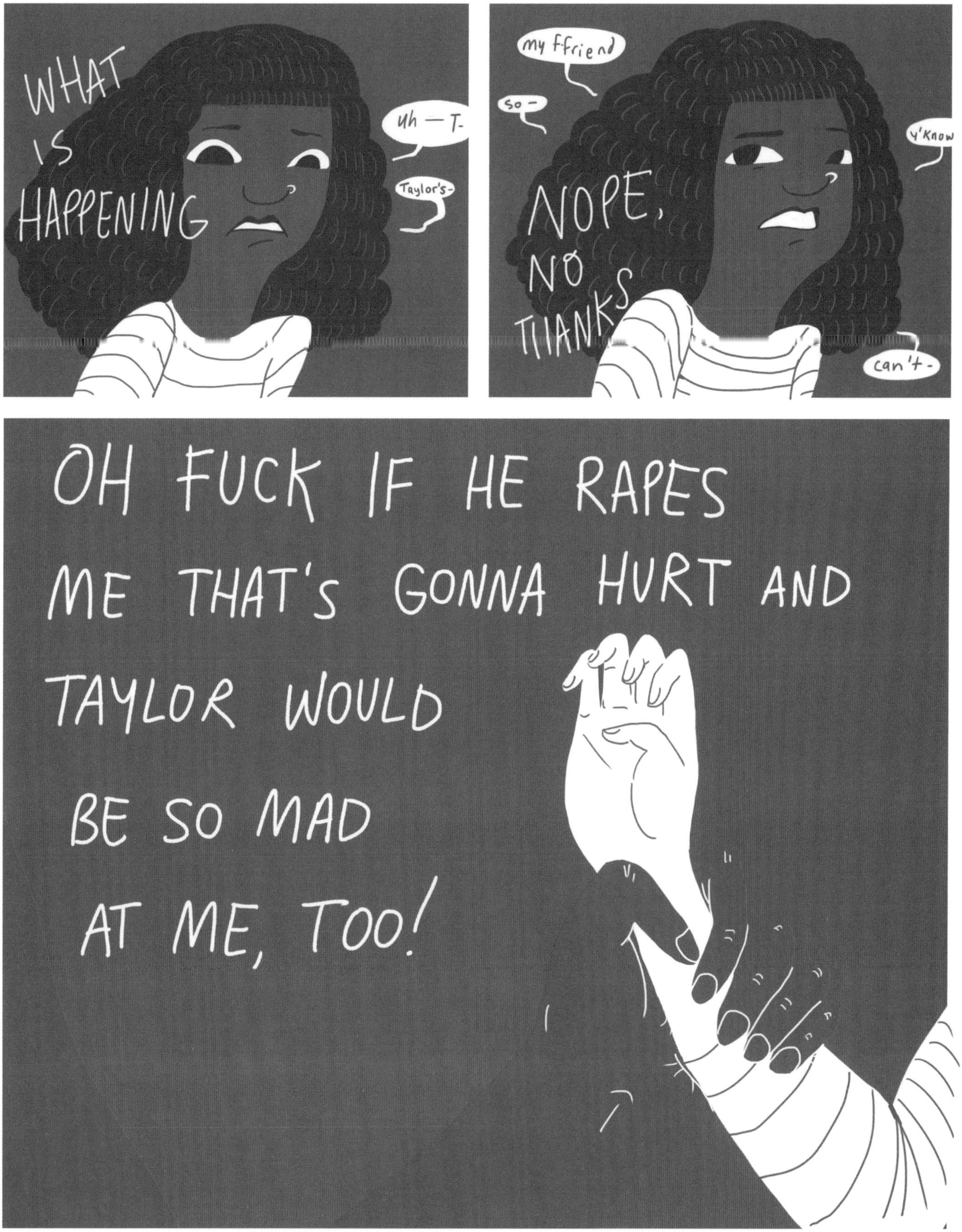
WHAT IS HAPPENING
uh — T-
Taylor's-
my ffriend
so -
y'Know
NOPE, NO THANKS
can't-
OH FUCK IF HE RAPES ME THAT'S GONNA HURT AND TAYLOR WOULD BE SO MAD AT ME, TOO!

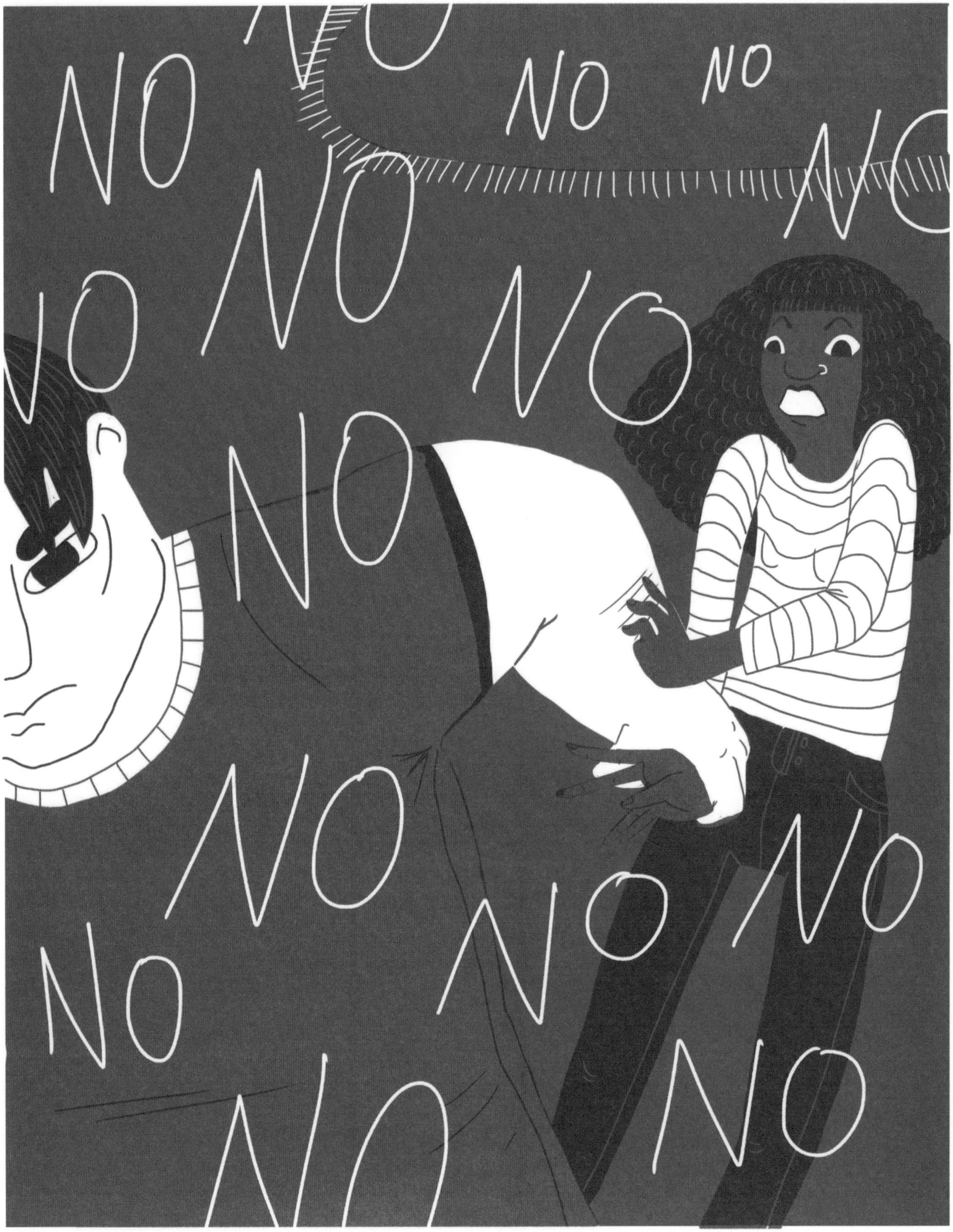
NO
NO
NO
NO
NO
NO
NO
NO
NO
NO
NO
NO
NO

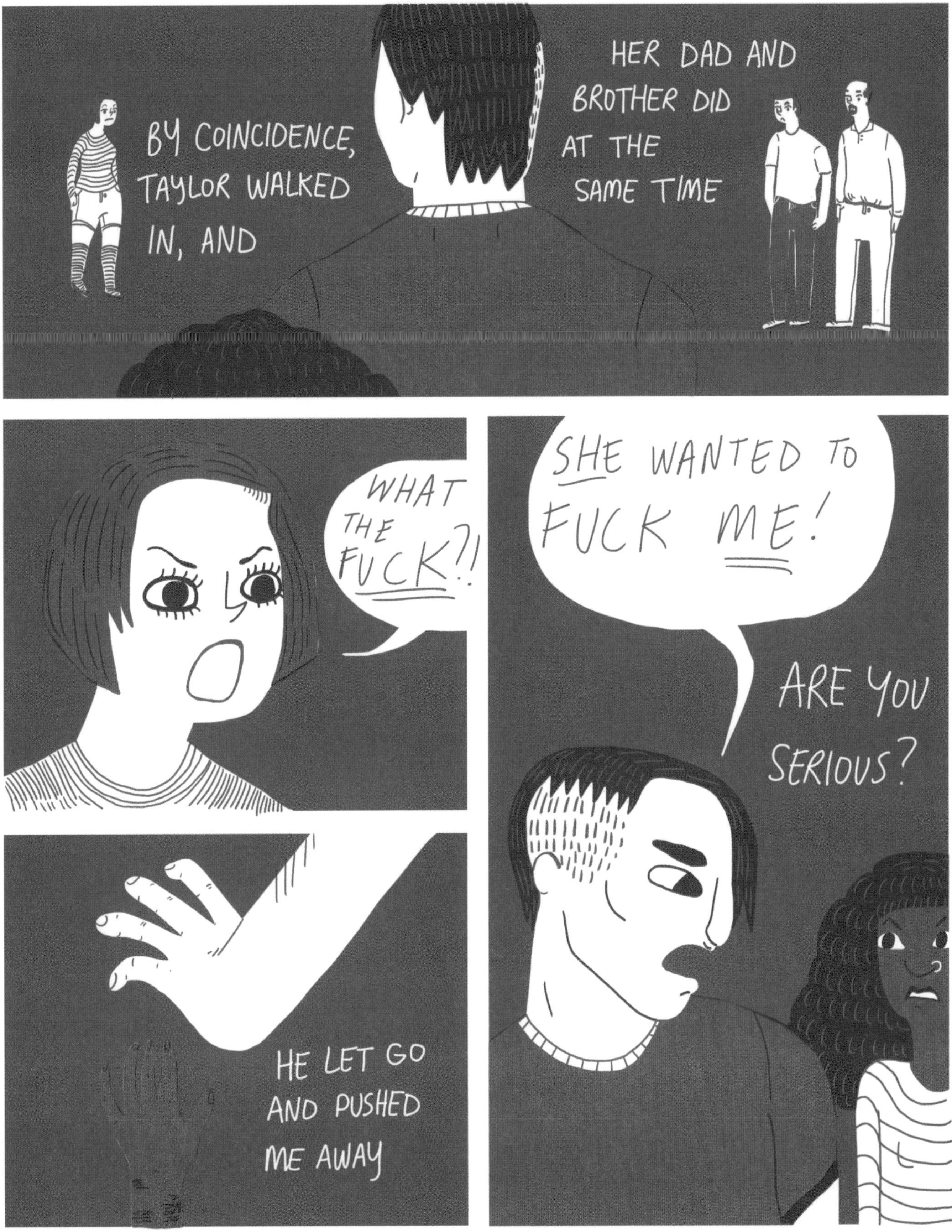
BY COINCIDENCE, TAYLOR WALKED IN, AND
HER DAD AND BROTHER DID AT THE SAME TIME
WHAT THE FUCK?!
SHE WANTED TO FUCK ME!
ARE YOU SERIOUS?
HE LET GO AND PUSHED ME AWAY

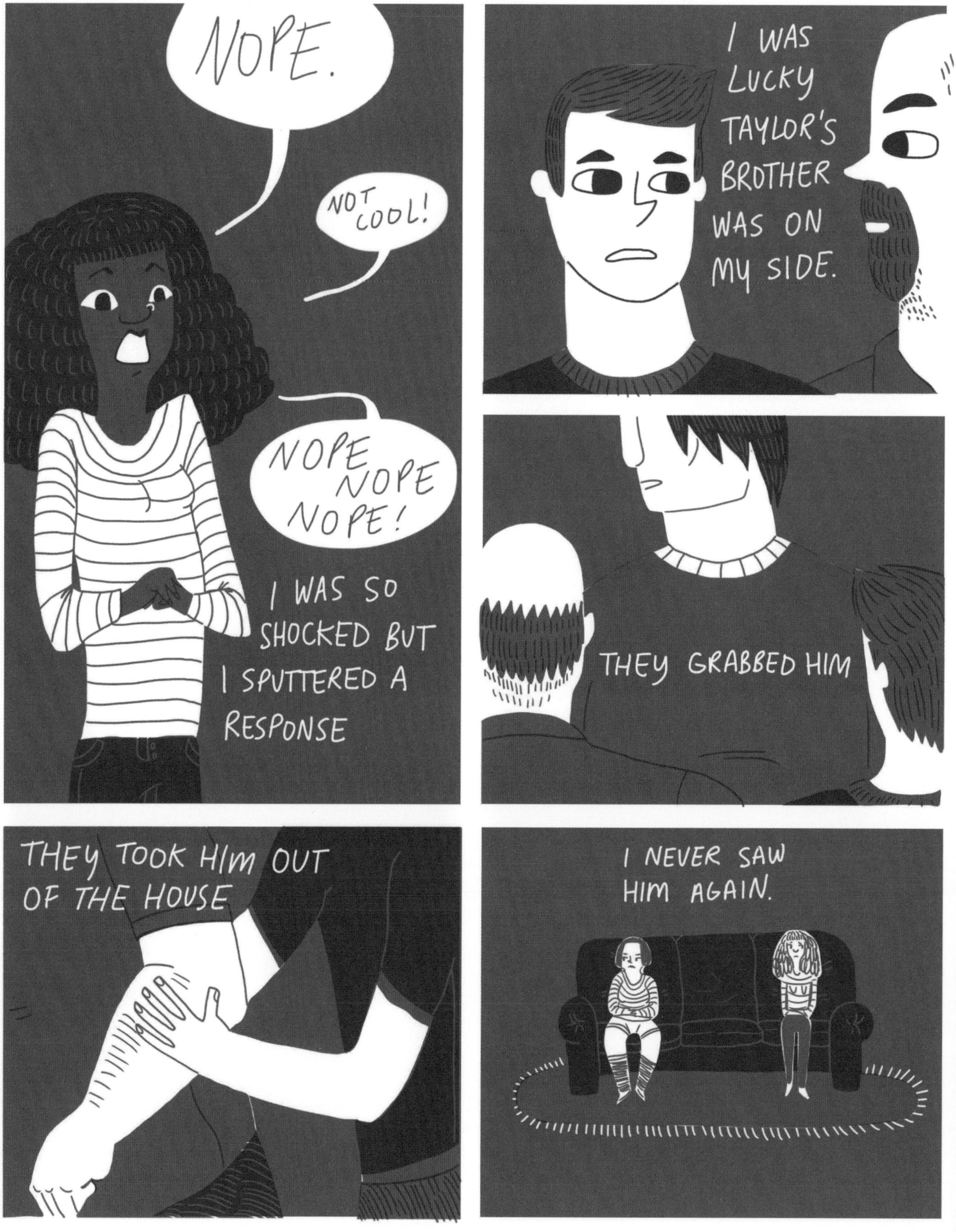

NOPE.
NOT COOL!
NOPE NOPE NOPE!
I WAS SO SHOCKED BUT I SPUTTERED A RESPONSE
I WAS LUCKY TAYLOR'S BROTHER WAS ON MY SIDE.
THEY GRABBED HIM
THEY TOOK HIM OUT OF THE HOUSE
I NEVER SAW HIM AGAIN.

TEN

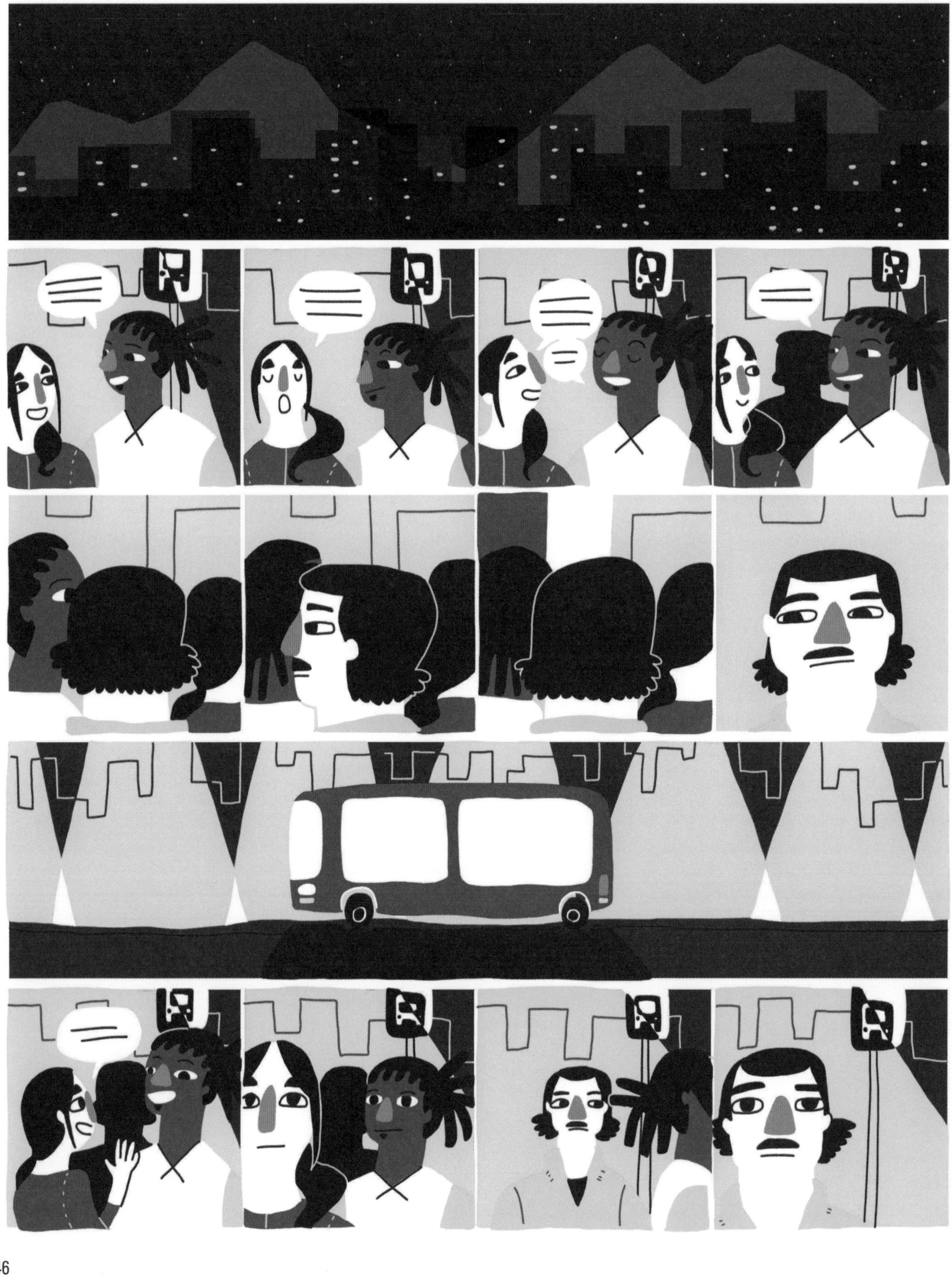

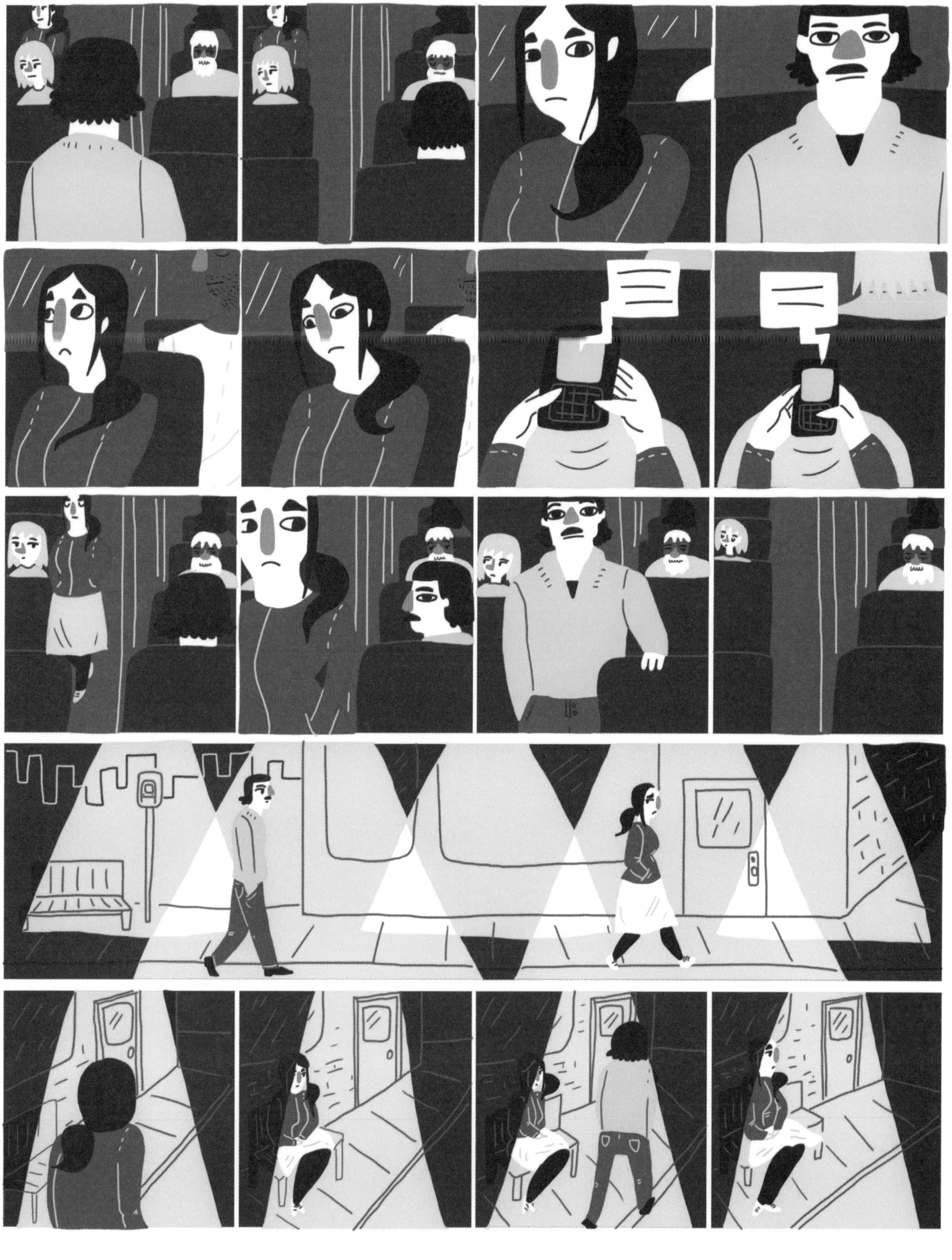

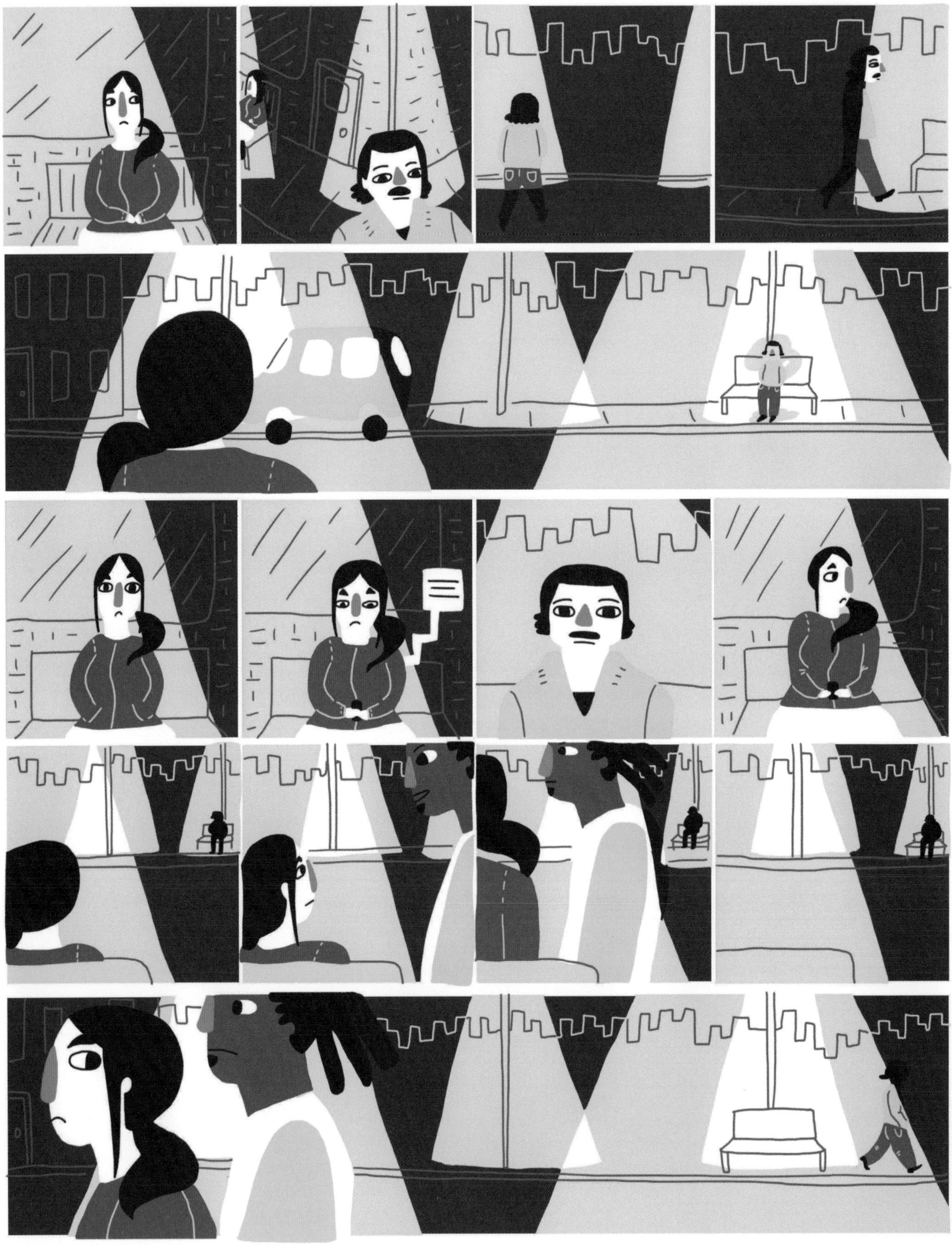

ELEVEN

We met on Nexopia, and really hit it off. We would alternate going back and forth by Greyhound. His friends came down one time. They were playing games in the basement and I'd asked him to clean up his dishes. He kept ignoring me so I put my hand in front of his computer screen.

That was the first time he hit me. Sent my glasses flying about ten feet. I was in shock. I'd never been slapped across the face before and told to fuck off. So I picked them up, and picked up the dishes.

The next day he asked if I understood why he hit me. I said no, so I got a half hour long lecture about how when he's playing games with his friends he's not to be interrupted. So I said ok, I understood.

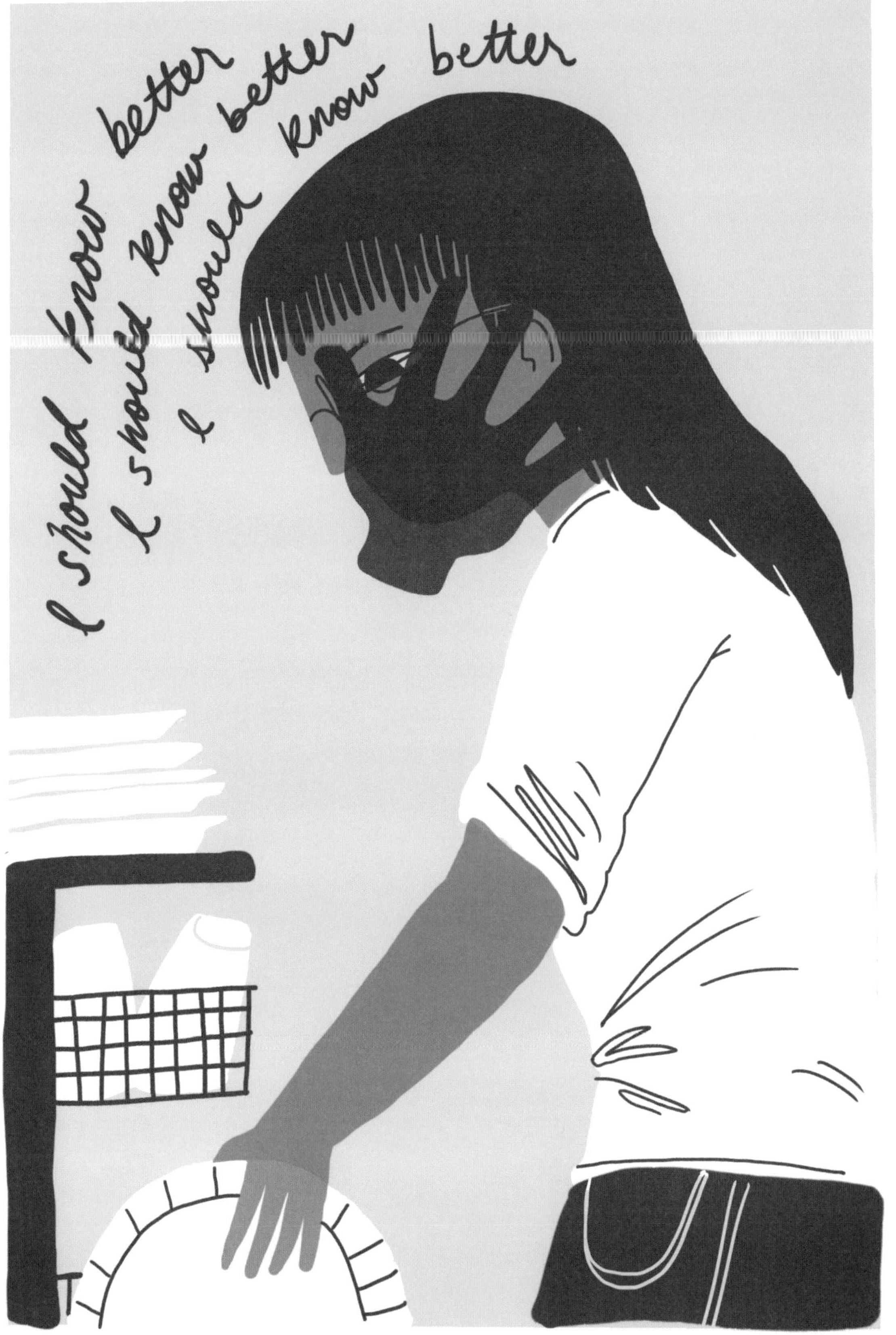
I should know better
I should know better
I should know better

⟨I didn't realize how hard it would be to... actually, physically record what had happened.⟩

I was doing some laundry, and he kept harassing me for sex. I'd said no, not right now, I'm busy. Pestering, harassing, it was getting really frustrating. I bent over to grab the laundry and he held me down. I told him, knock it off, this wasn't funny. He grabbed my arms, held them behind my back and pulled my pants down.

There is nothing more terrifying than having someone you trust hold you down after you say no and start crying. The feeling of complete and utter betrayal and helplessness. To have someone hold you there, and rape you. Rape you and tell you to stop crying and just enjoy it. Stop crying, enjoy it. I remember the words exactly. Enjoy it.
There's nothing you can compare it to. Nothing.

I cried. A lot. I had a shower after. I'd scrubbed my whole body raw, I felt disgusting. Dirty, filthy. I felt like nothing.

But I showered, and just continued on my way. Because when it happened I didn't consider it rape. We were dating after all. He was allowed to do that. Right?

He moved in. He wanted sex every night, and I was too tired to fight it by the end of the day. We got a kitty in the interim. I didn't really like the name he chose but I loved her nonetheless.

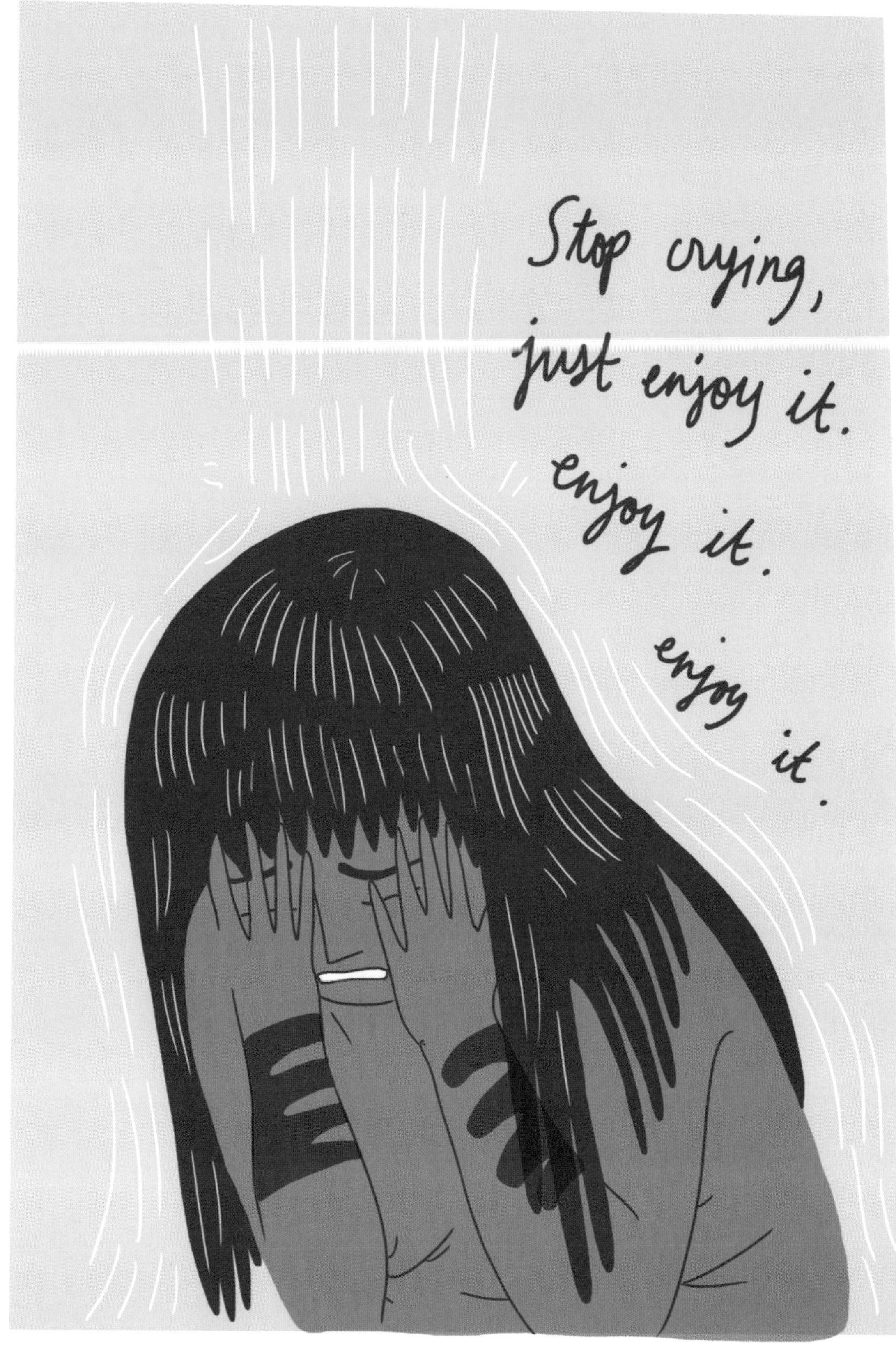
Stop crying,
just enjoy it.
enjoy it.
enjoy it.

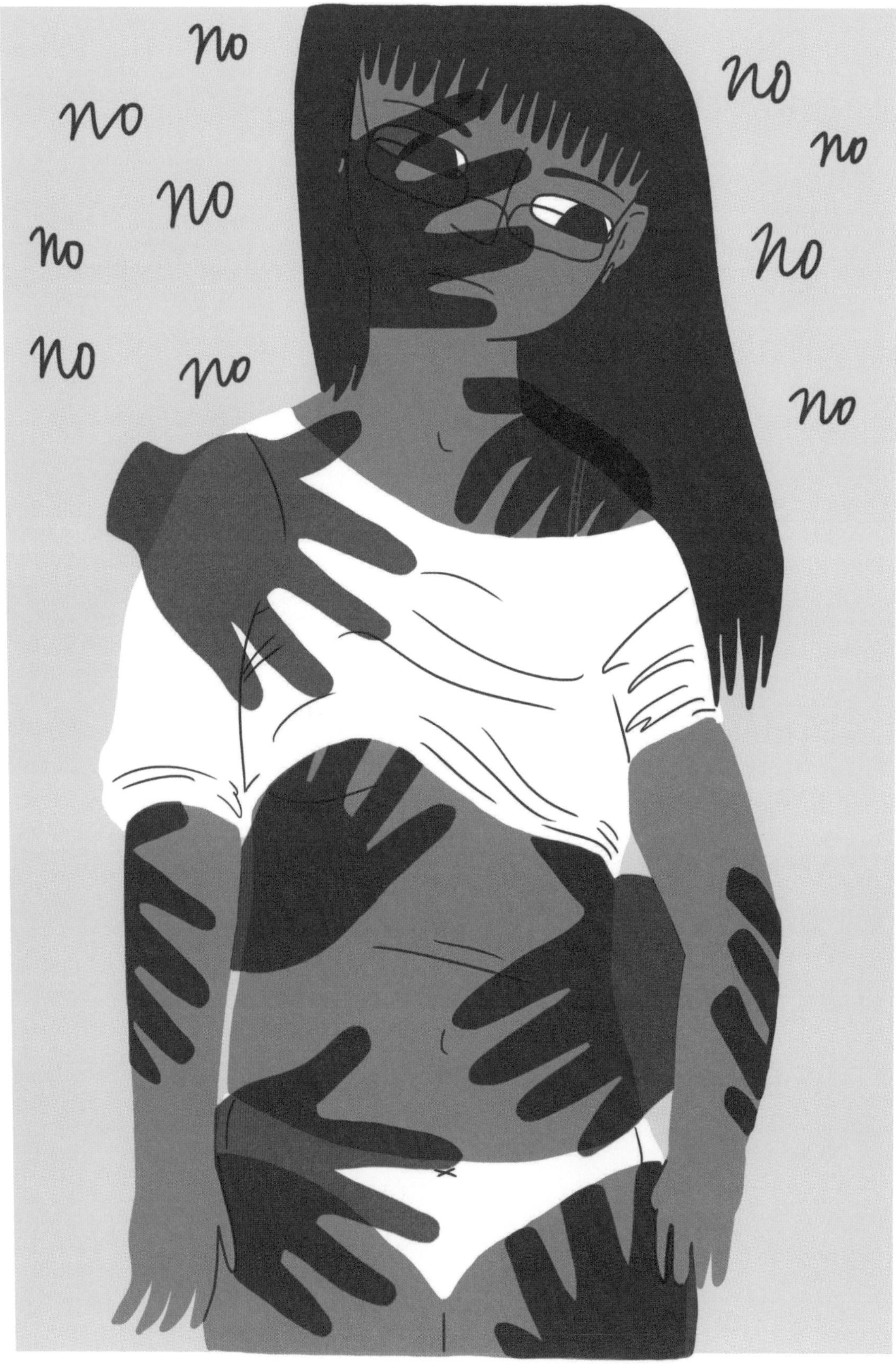
no
no
no
no
no
no
no
no
no
no
no

Meanwhile he'd been deleting messages from my friends, friend requests on Facebook, emails, cancelling my plans and my mail subscriptions on my behalf. Would I admit it? No.

Thanksgiving: We went to my grandparents', we were all having fun, we were even teasing each other.

Then he slapped me across the face. In front of seven family members.

After we got home from Thanksgiving, I told him to get the fuck out. If he wasn't out of the apartment by the time I was done work I was calling the cops.

When I got home he was gone. Everything was different.
That was the most peaceful sleep I had gotten in a very, very long time.

I renamed my cat. Her name is Lucy. She reminds me of that time, that time I didn't trust my instincts.

He had taken my friends. My family. My freedom.
Never again.

Did that relationship affect my life? It's been five years and I haven't been in a relationshp since.

TWELVE

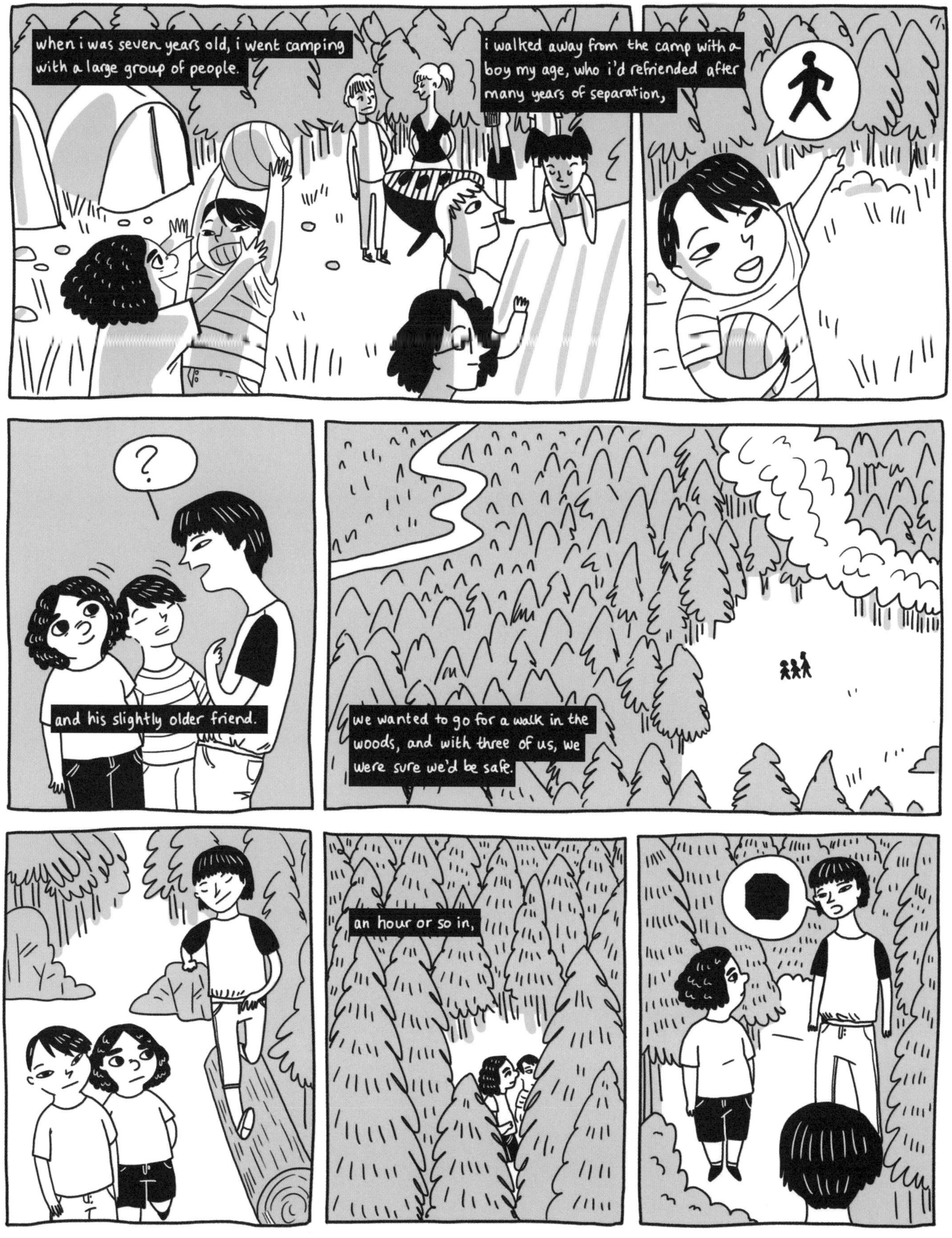
when i was seven years old, i went camping with a large group of people.
i walked away from the camp with a boy my age, who i'd refriended after many years of separation,
?
and his slightly older friend.
we wanted to go for a walk in the woods, and with three of us, we were sure we'd be safe.
an hour or so in,

the older boy had to pee.

zzzip!

i turned and covered my eyes, embarassed, and he laughed at my modesty.

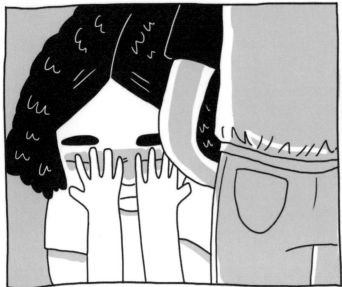

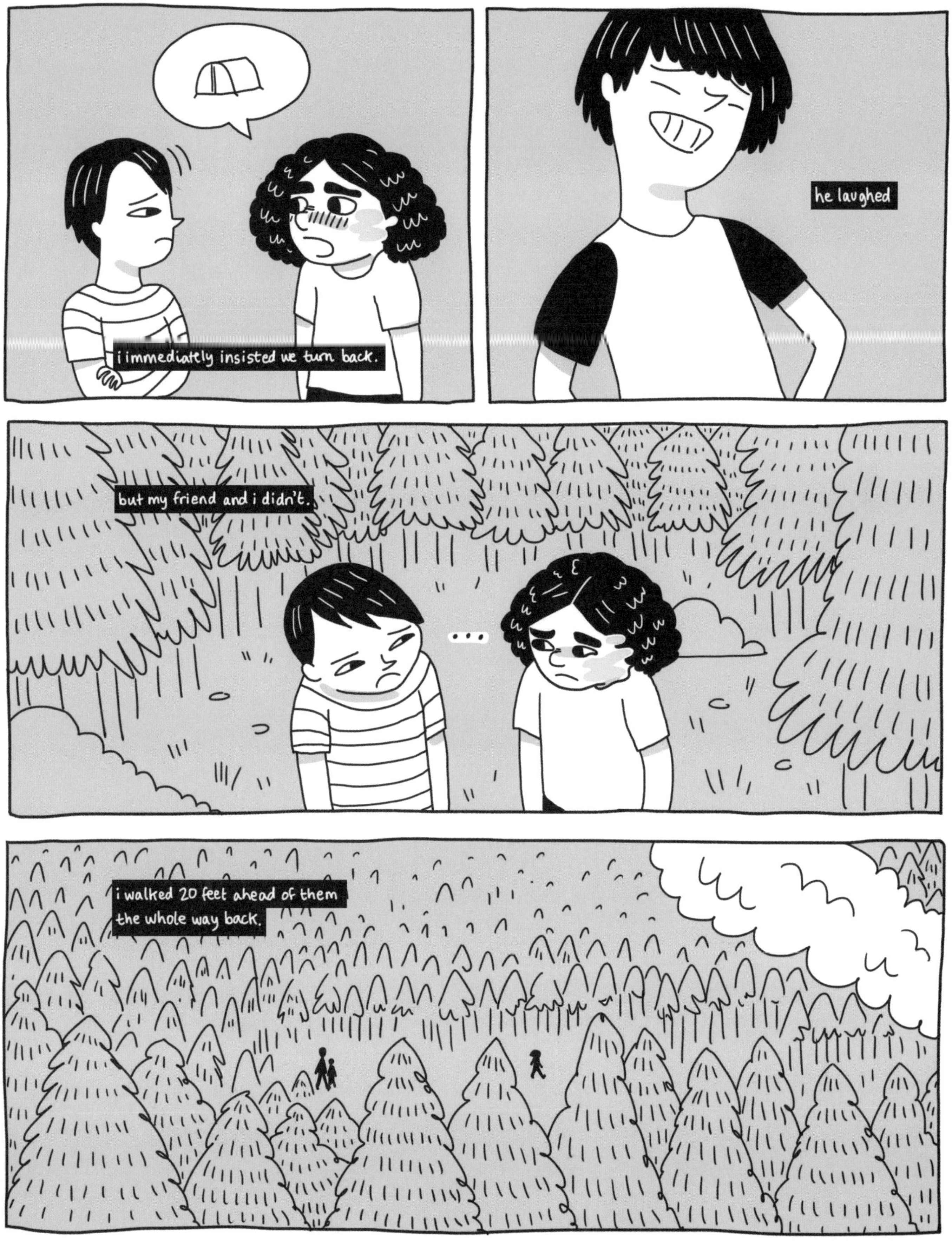
i immediatly insisted we turn back.
he laughed
but my friend and i didn't.
...
i walked 20 feet ahead of them
the whole way back.

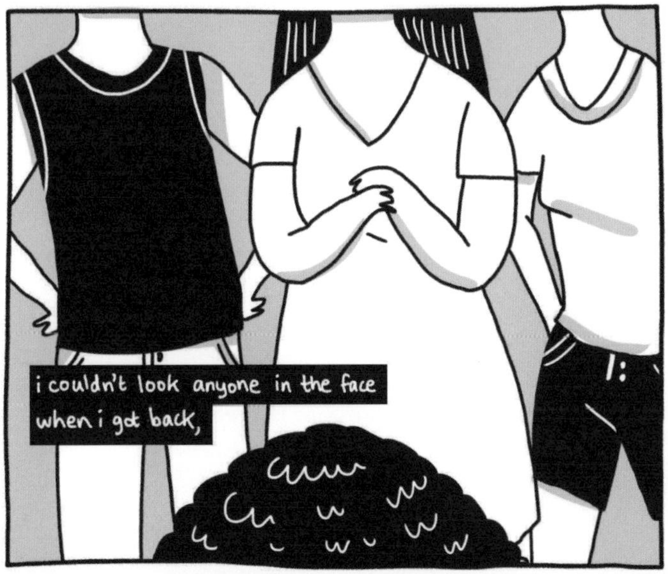
i couldn't look anyone in the face
when i got back,

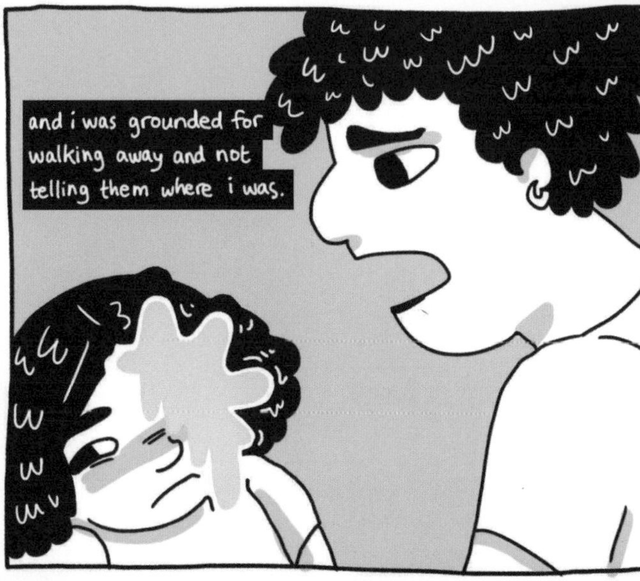
and i was grounded for
walking away and not
telling them where i was.

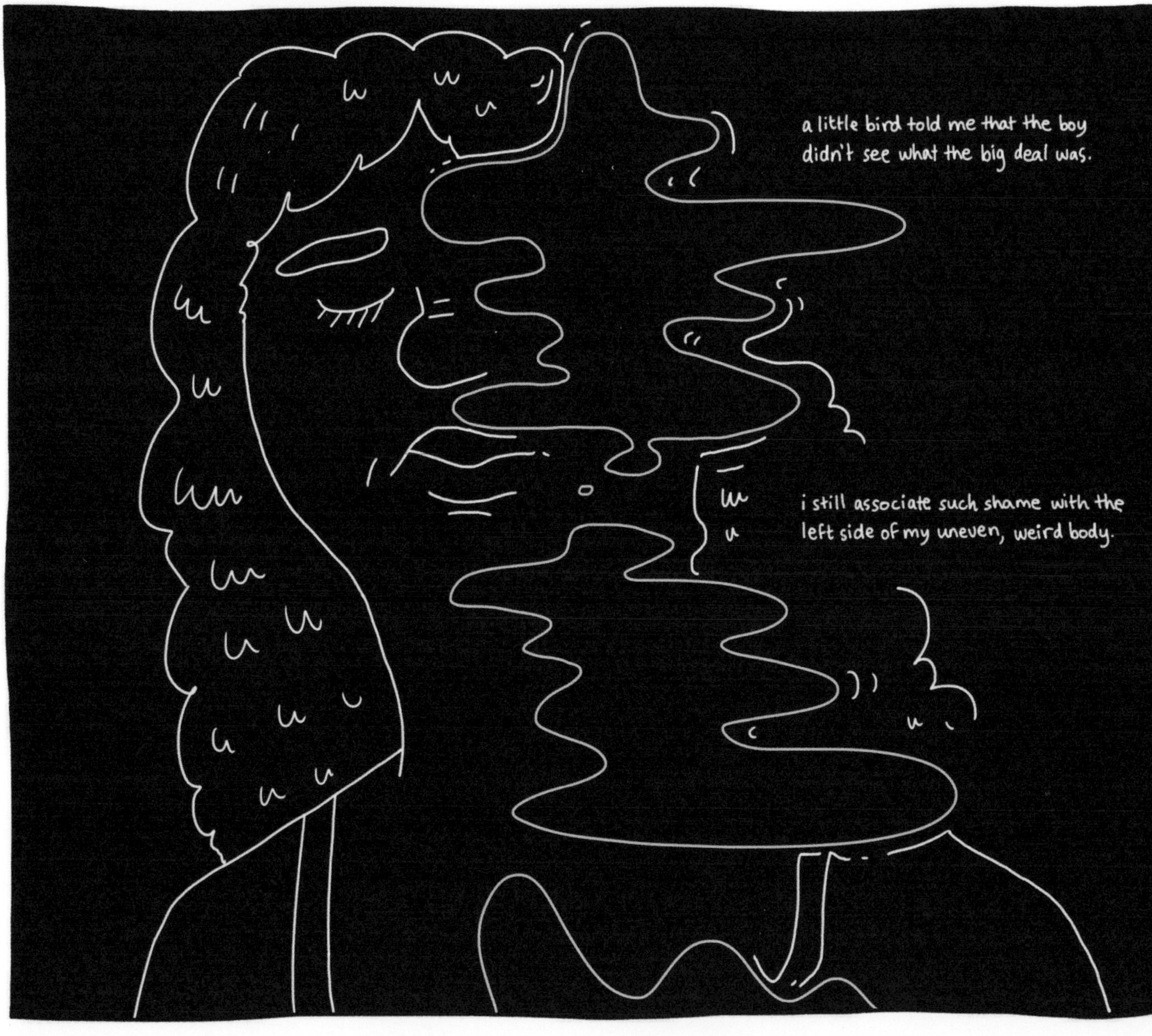
a little bird told me that the boy
didn't see what the big deal was.
i still associate such shame with the
left side of my uneven, weird body.

THIRTEEN

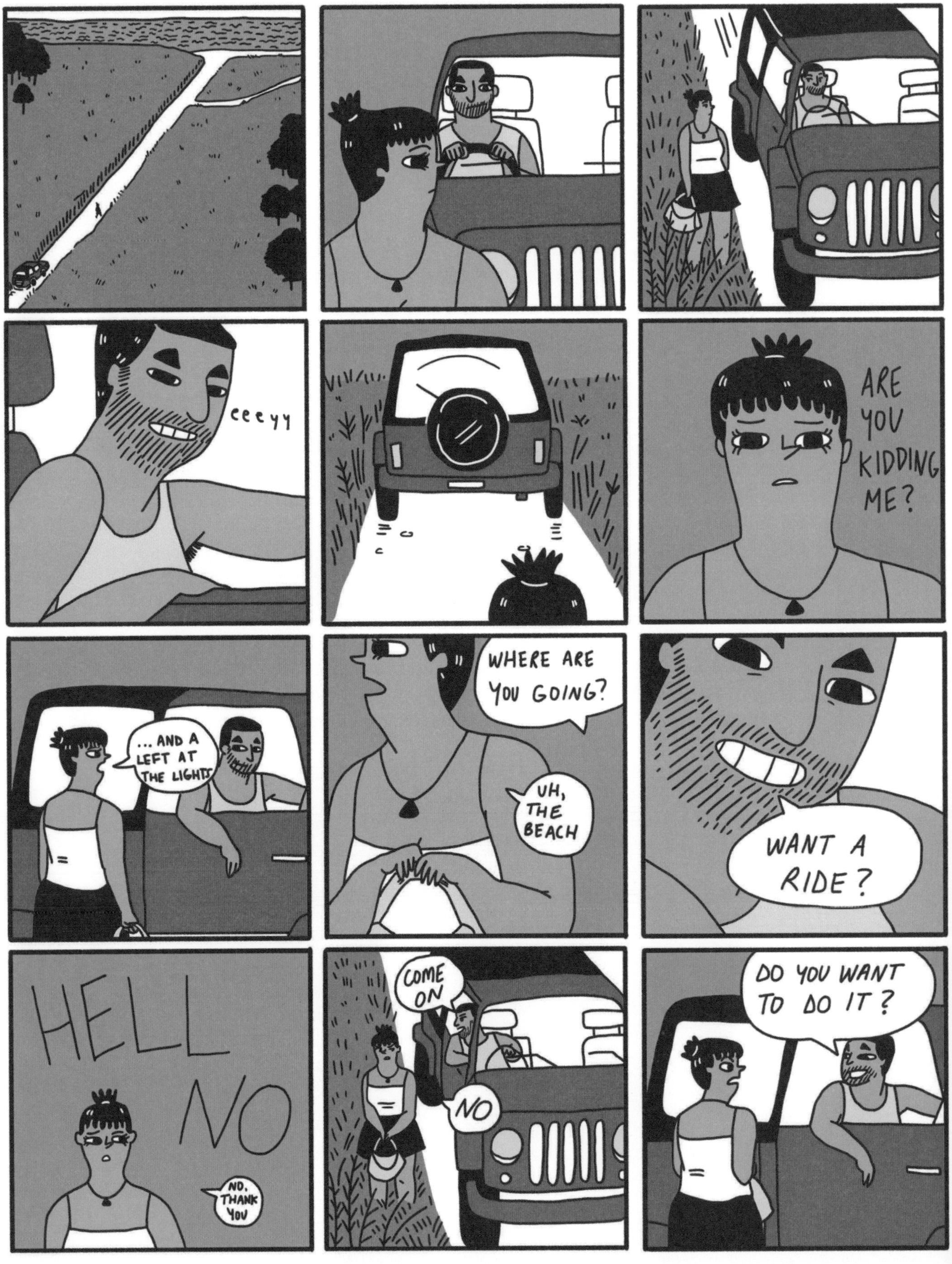

eeeyy
ARE YOU KIDDING ME?
... AND A LEFT AT THE LIGHTS
WHERE ARE YOU GOING?
UH, THE BEACH
WANT A RIDE?
HELL NO
NO, THANK YOU
COME ON
NO
DO YOU WANT TO DO IT?

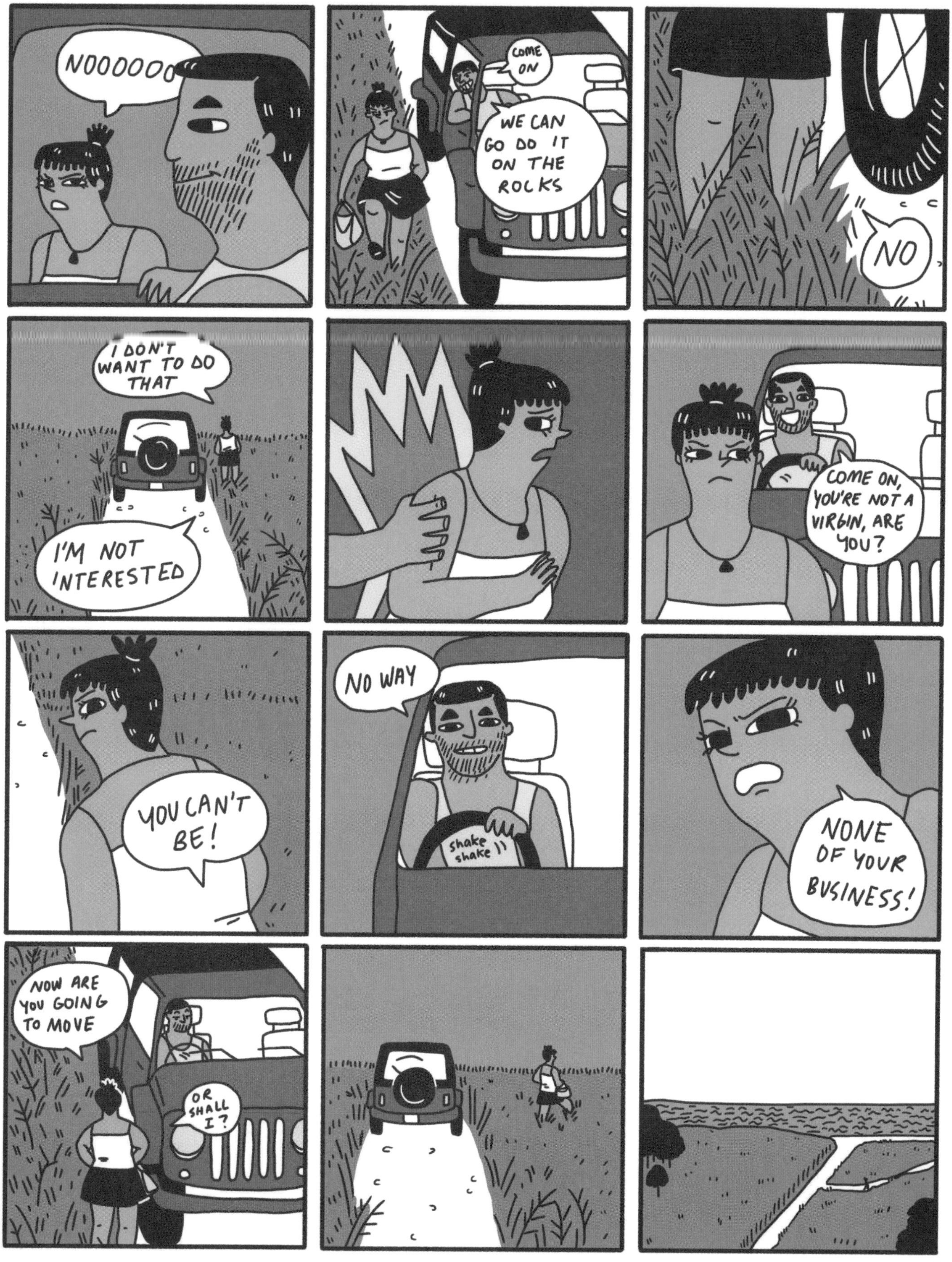
NOOOOOO
COME ON
WE CAN GO DO IT ON THE ROCKS
NO
I DON'T WANT TO DO THAT
I'M NOT INTERESTED
COME ON, YOU'RE NOT A VIRGIN, ARE YOU?
YOU CAN'T BE!
NO WAY
shake shake
NONE OF YOUR BUSINESS!
NOW ARE YOU GOING TO MOVE
OR SHALL I?

FOURTEEN

SAN FRANCISCO

BY
NICE HAIR, BABY
HOW DO YOU GET IT LIKE THAT?
AW, DON'T BE LIKE THAT, HONEY

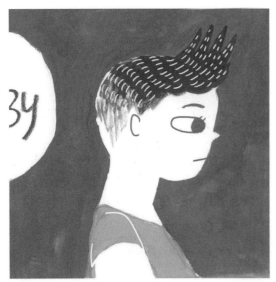

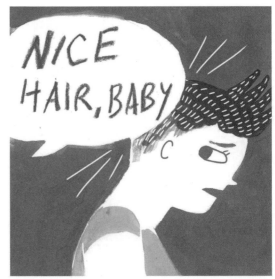

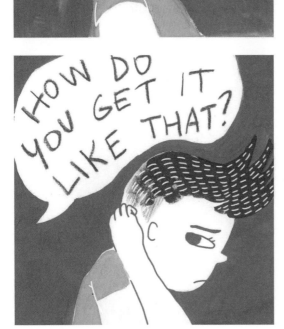

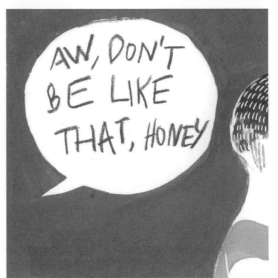

1

HEY!
MY FRIEND LIKES YOUR HAIR, YOU SHOULD ASK HIM OUT!
WOW, SHE DIDN'T EVEN LOOK AT YOU!
OSCAR THE GROUCH
OSCAR THE GROUCH
OSCAR THE GROUCH
OSCAR THE GROUC

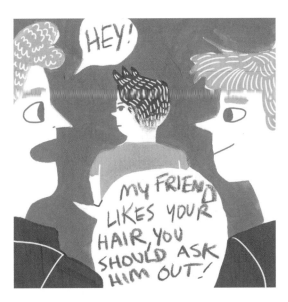

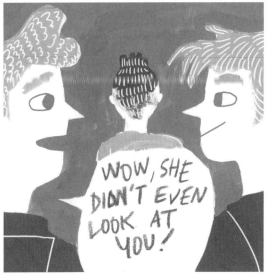

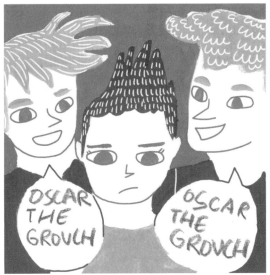

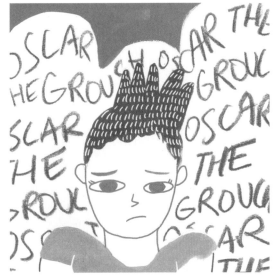

2

I BET NO ONE WOULD NOTICE IF WE GRABBED HER
HA-HA, YEAH
HAH!
HAHA

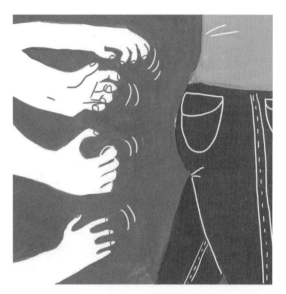

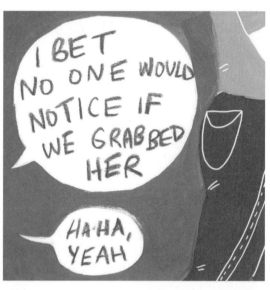

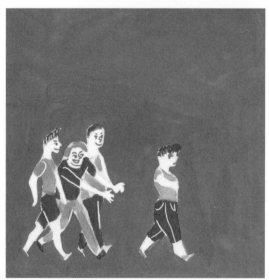

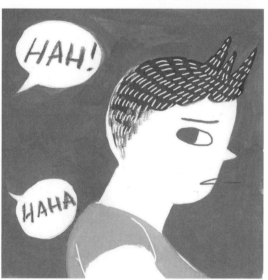

3

FIFTEEN

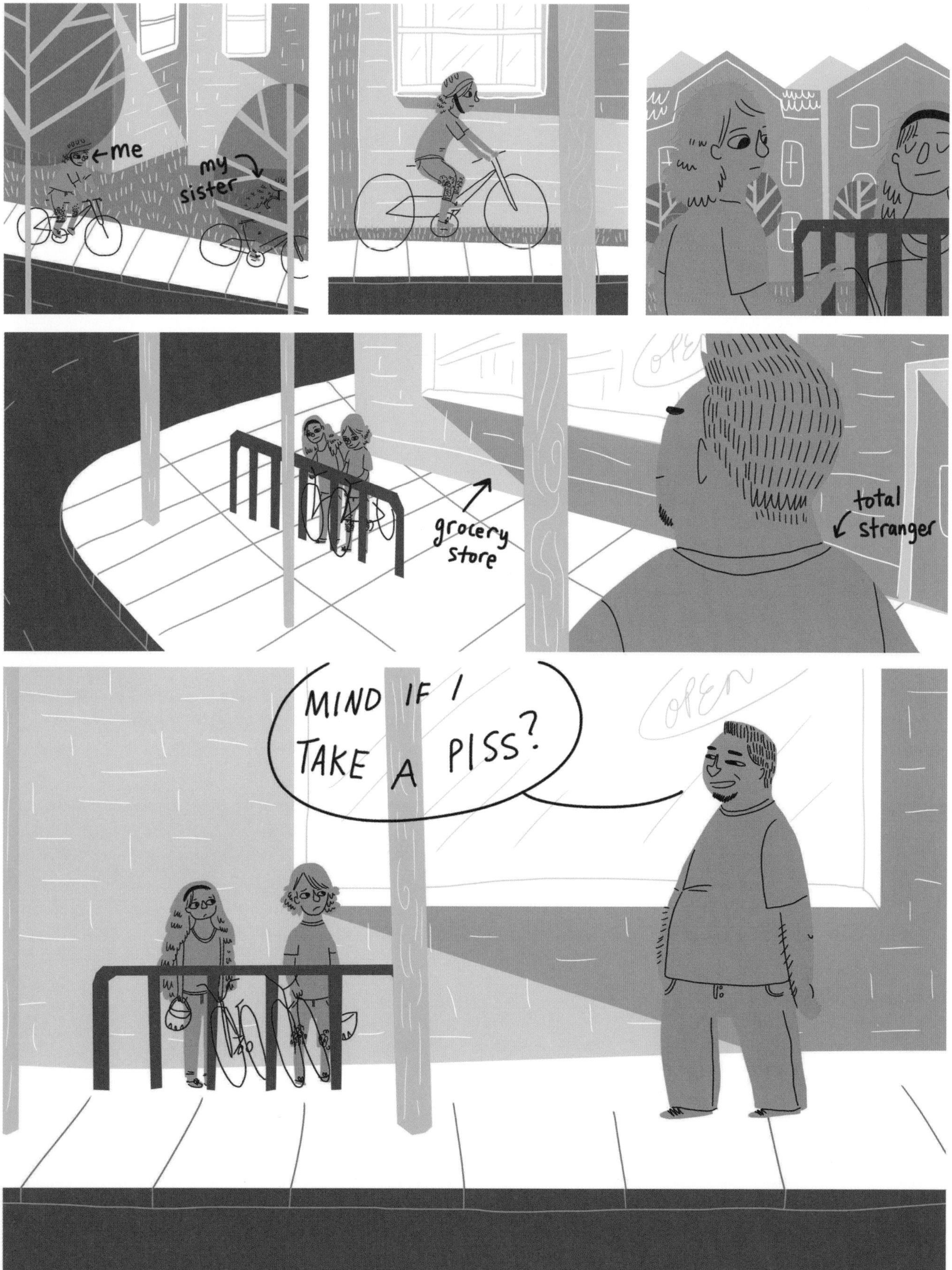
←me
my sister
grocery store
total stranger
MIND IF I TAKE A PISS?

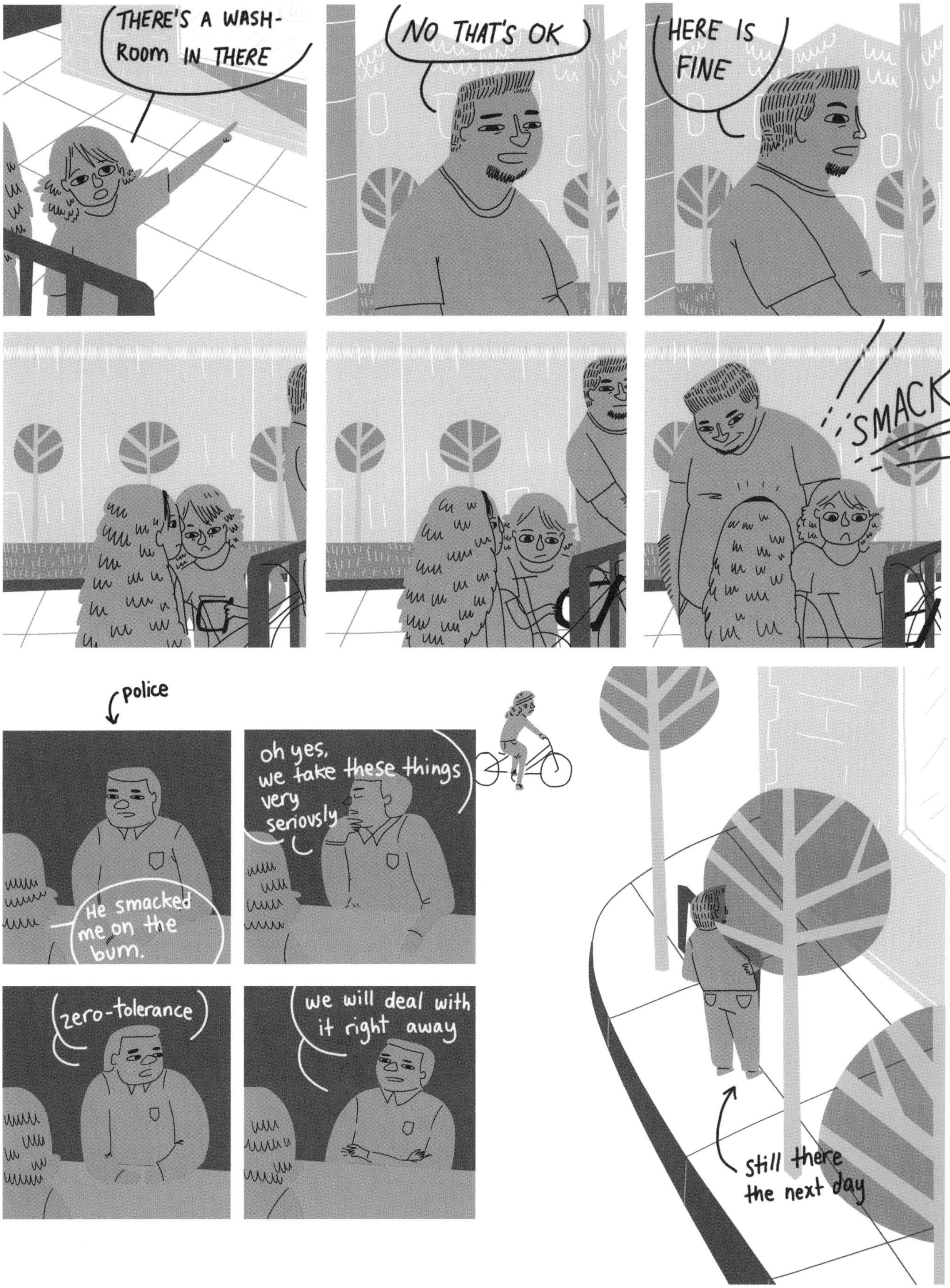
THERE'S A WASH-ROOM IN THERE
NO THAT'S OK
HERE IS FINE
SMACK!
police
He smacked me on the bum.
oh yes, we take these things very seriously
zero-tolerance
we will deal with it right away
still there the next day

SIXTEEN

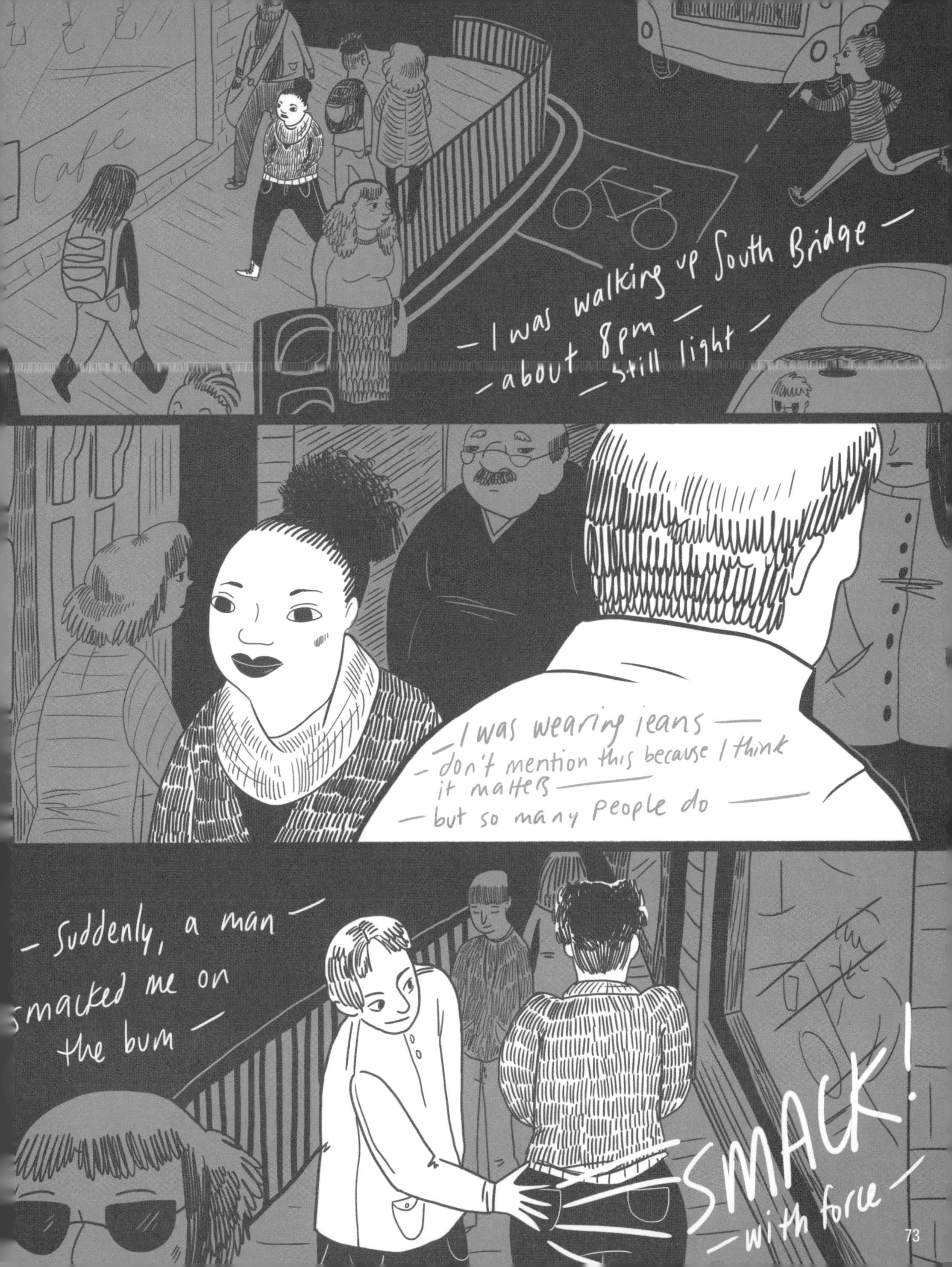
Café
— I was walking up South Bridge —
— about 8pm —
— still light —
— I was wearing jeans —
— don't mention this because I think it matters —
— but so many people do —
— Suddenly, a man smacked me on the bum —
SMACK!
— with force —

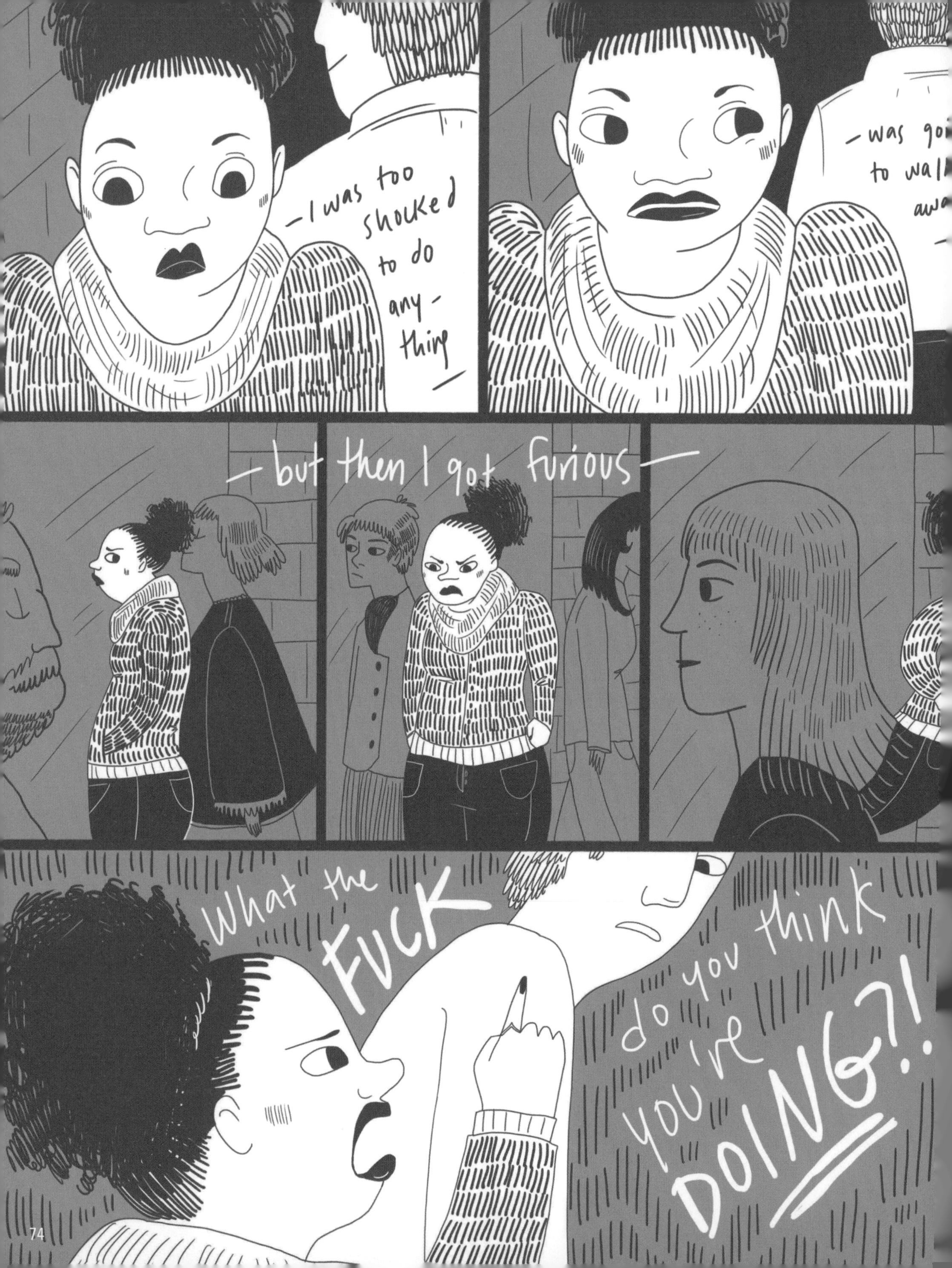
—I was too shocked to do any-thing—
—was goi to wal awa
—but then I got furious—
What the FUCK do you think you're DOING?!

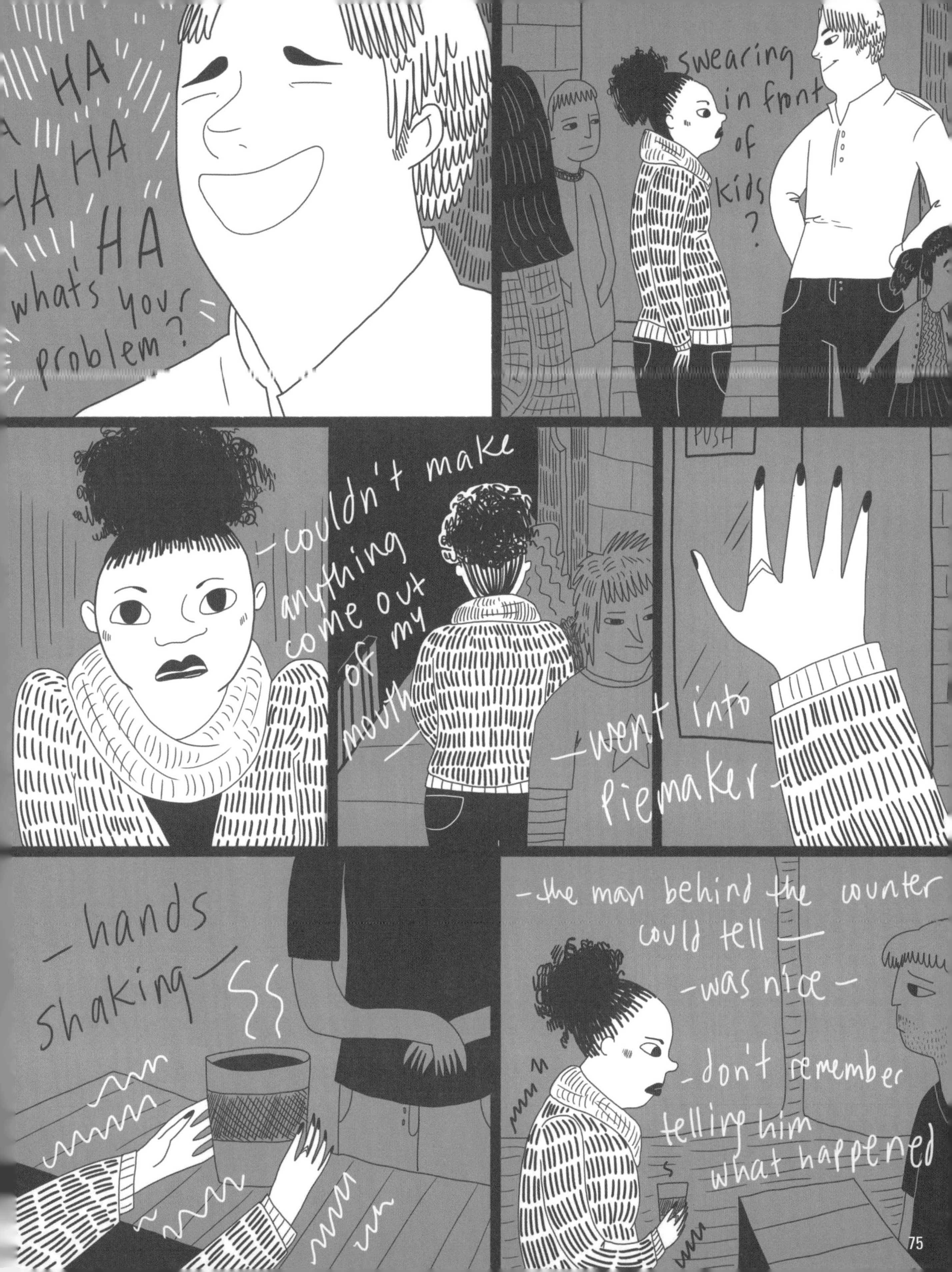
HA HA HA HA HA
what's your problem?
swearing in front of kids?
—couldn't make anything come out of my mouth—
PUSH
—went into Piemaker—
—hands shaking—
—the man behind the counter could tell—
—was nice—
—don't remember telling him what happened

SEVENTEEN

I WAS IN GRADE TWELVE AND IT WAS
GRAD CAMP-OUT NIGHT.

WE WERE DRUNK, WE MADE OUT.

HE WAS MY FRIEND.

WE WENT INTO SOME BUSHES AND HE
WOUND UP ON TOP OF ME.

HANDS IN MY UNDERWEAR, TOUCHING ME.

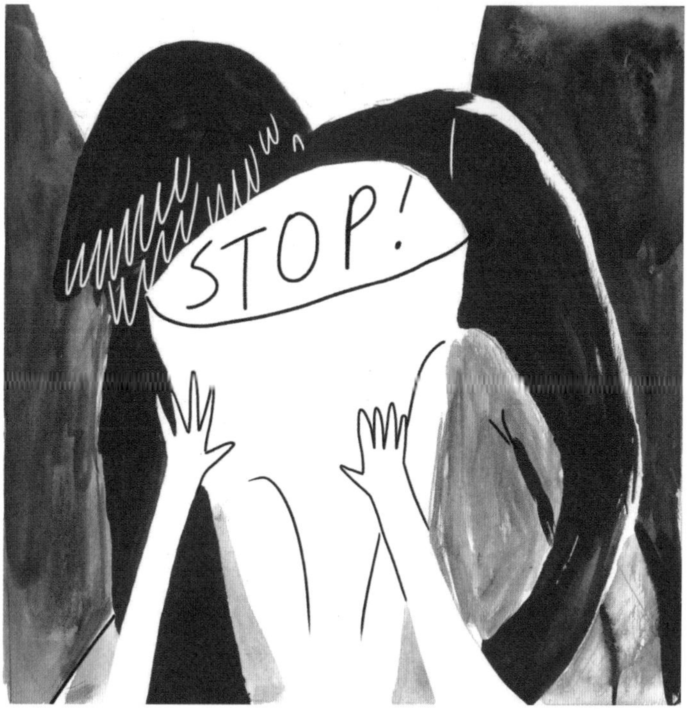
STOP!

I TOLD HIM TO STOP AND HE DIDN'T, BUT I WAS TOO DRUNK AND LITTLE TO GET AWAY.

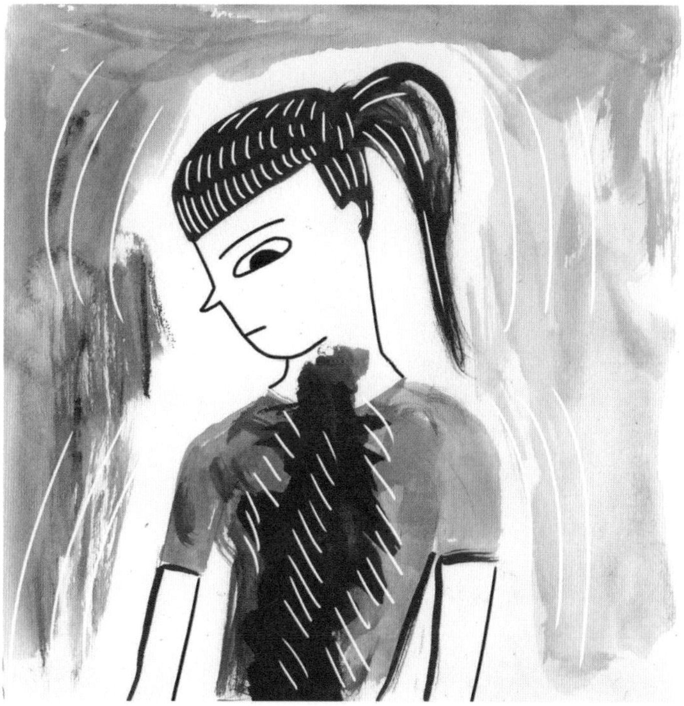

IT TOOK ME A FEW DAYS TO FIGURE OUT WHAT WAS WRONG.

I CALLED HIM AND WE MET UP.

I TOLD HIM WHAT HE DID WAS WRONG AND TO NEVER DO IT TO ANYONE ELSE AGAIN.

I HAVEN'T SEEN HIM SINCE.

I HOPE HE LISTENED.

EIGHTEEN

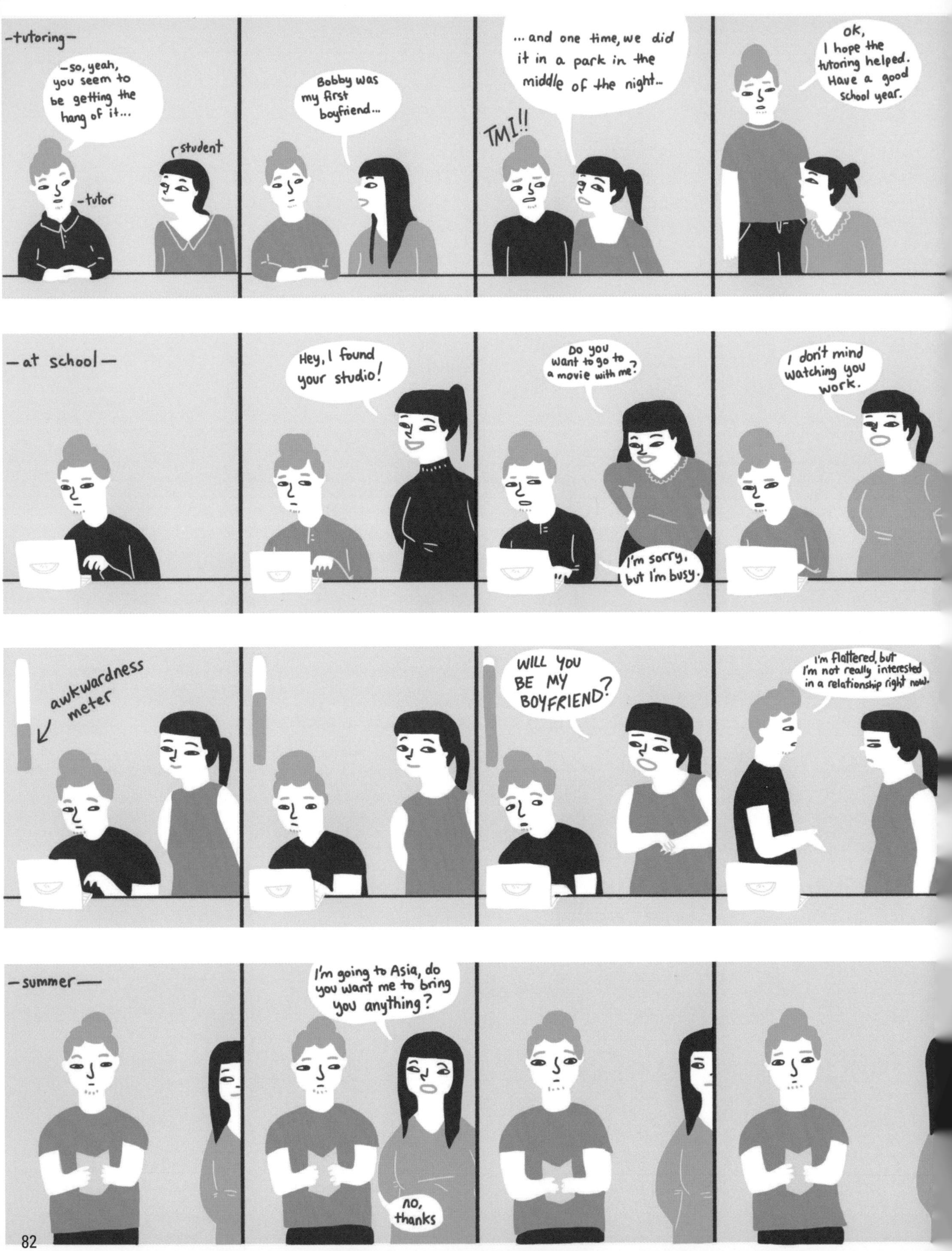
-tutoring-
-so, yeah, you seem to be getting the hang of it...
student
-tutor
Bobby was my first boyfriend...
...and one time, we did it in a park in the middle of the night...
TMI!!
ok, I hope the tutoring helped. Have a good school year.
-at school-
Hey, I found your studio!
Do you want to go to a movie with me?
I'm sorry, but I'm busy.
I don't mind watching you work.
awkwardness meter
WILL YOU BE MY BOYFRIEND?
I'm flattered, but I'm not really interested in a relationship right now.
-summer-
I'm going to Asia, do you want me to bring you anything?
no, thanks

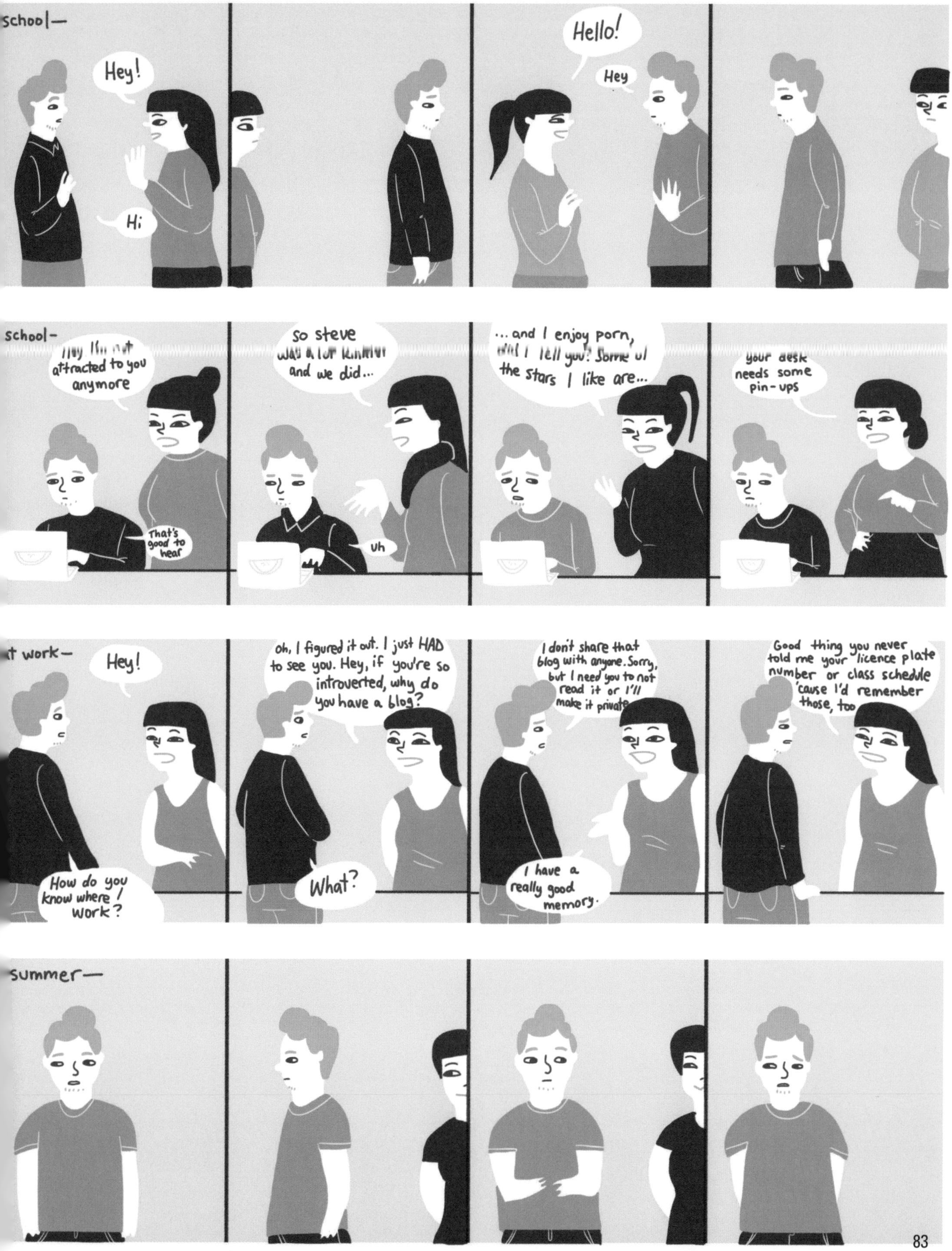
school—
Hey!
Hi
Hello!
Hey
school—
attracted to you anymore
That's good to hear
So steve
and we did...
Uh
...and I enjoy porn,
the stars I like are...
your desk needs some pin-ups
t work—
Hey!
How do you know where I work?
Oh, I figured it out. I just HAD to see you. Hey, if you're so introverted, why do you have a blog?
What?
I don't share that blog with anyone. Sorry, but I need you to not read it or I'll make it private
I have a really good memory.
Good thing you never told me your licence plate number or class schedule 'cause I'd remember those, too
summer—

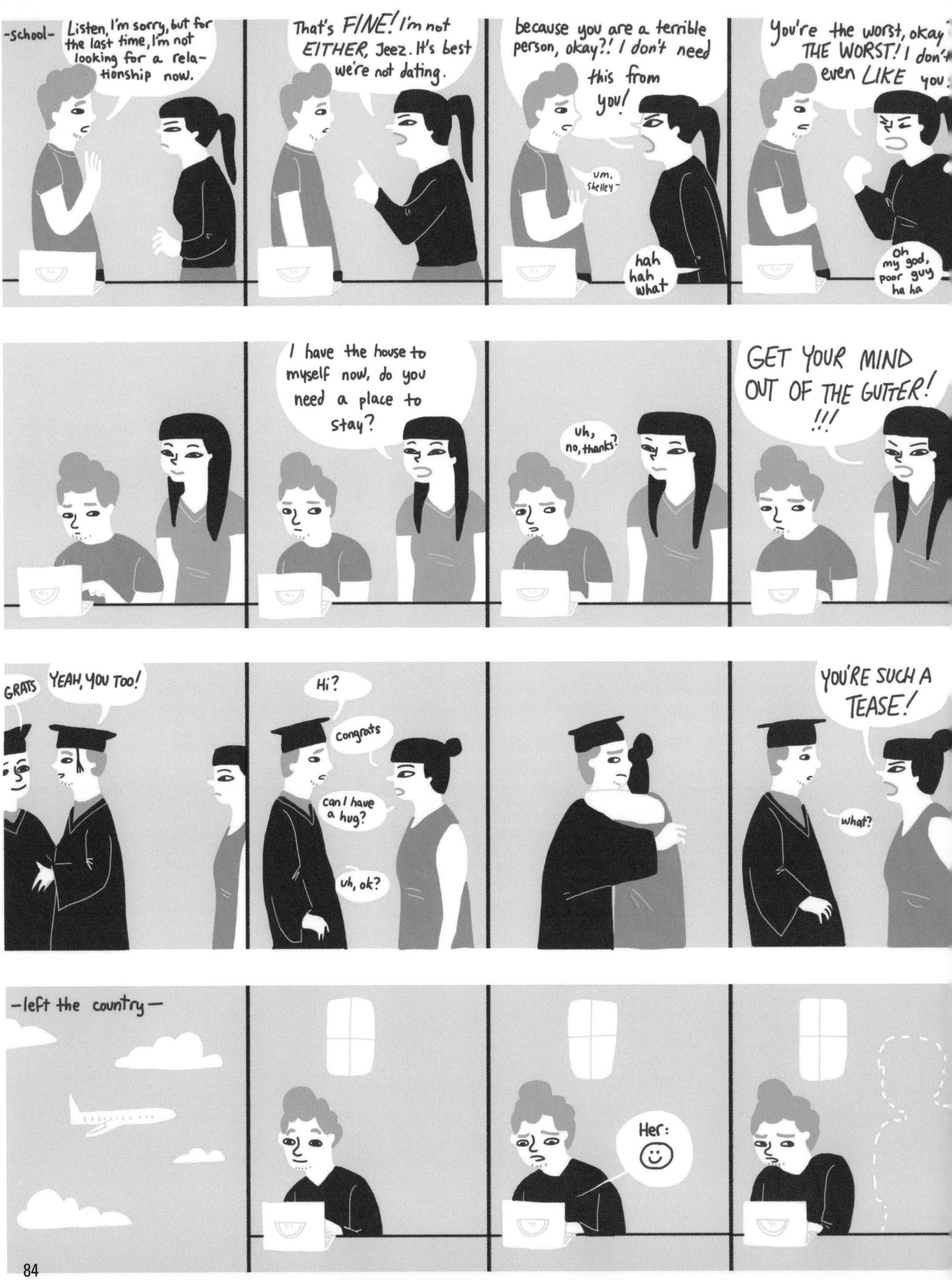

-school-
Listen, I'm sorry, but for the last time, I'm not looking for a relationship now.
That's FINE! I'm not EITHER, Jeez. It's best we're not dating.
because you are a terrible person, okay?! I don't need this from you!
um, Shelley-
hah hah what
You're the worst, okay THE WORST! I don't even LIKE you
Oh my god, poor guy ha ha
I have the house to myself now, do you need a place to stay?
Uh, no, thanks?
GET YOUR MIND OUT OF THE GUTTER! !!!
GRATS
YEAH, YOU TOO!
Hi?
congrats
can I have a hug?
uh, ok?
YOU'RE SUCH A TEASE!
what?
-left the country-
Her:

NINETEEN

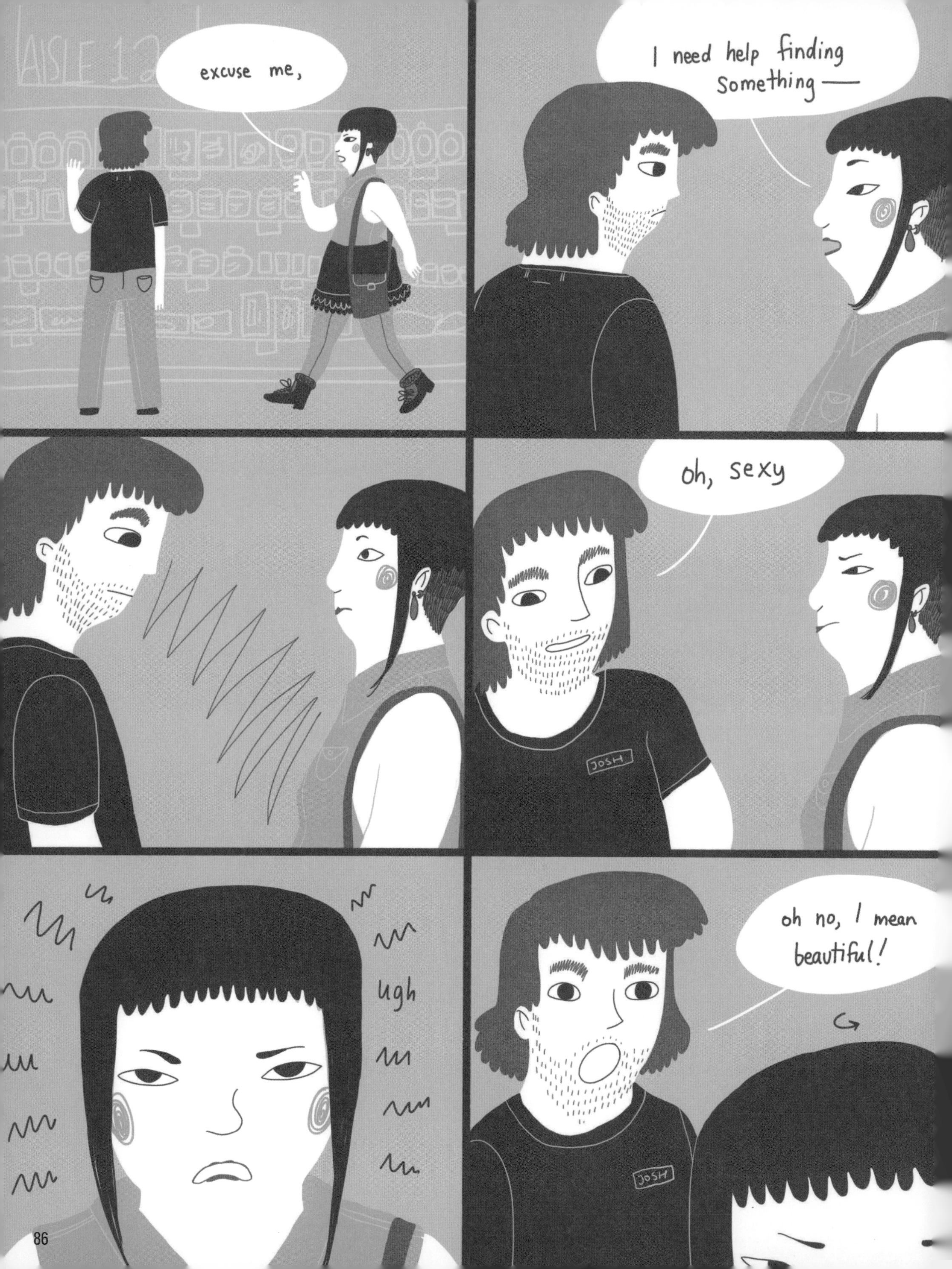
AISLE 12
excuse me,
I need help finding Something —
oh, sexy
ugh
oh no, I mean beautiful!
JOSH

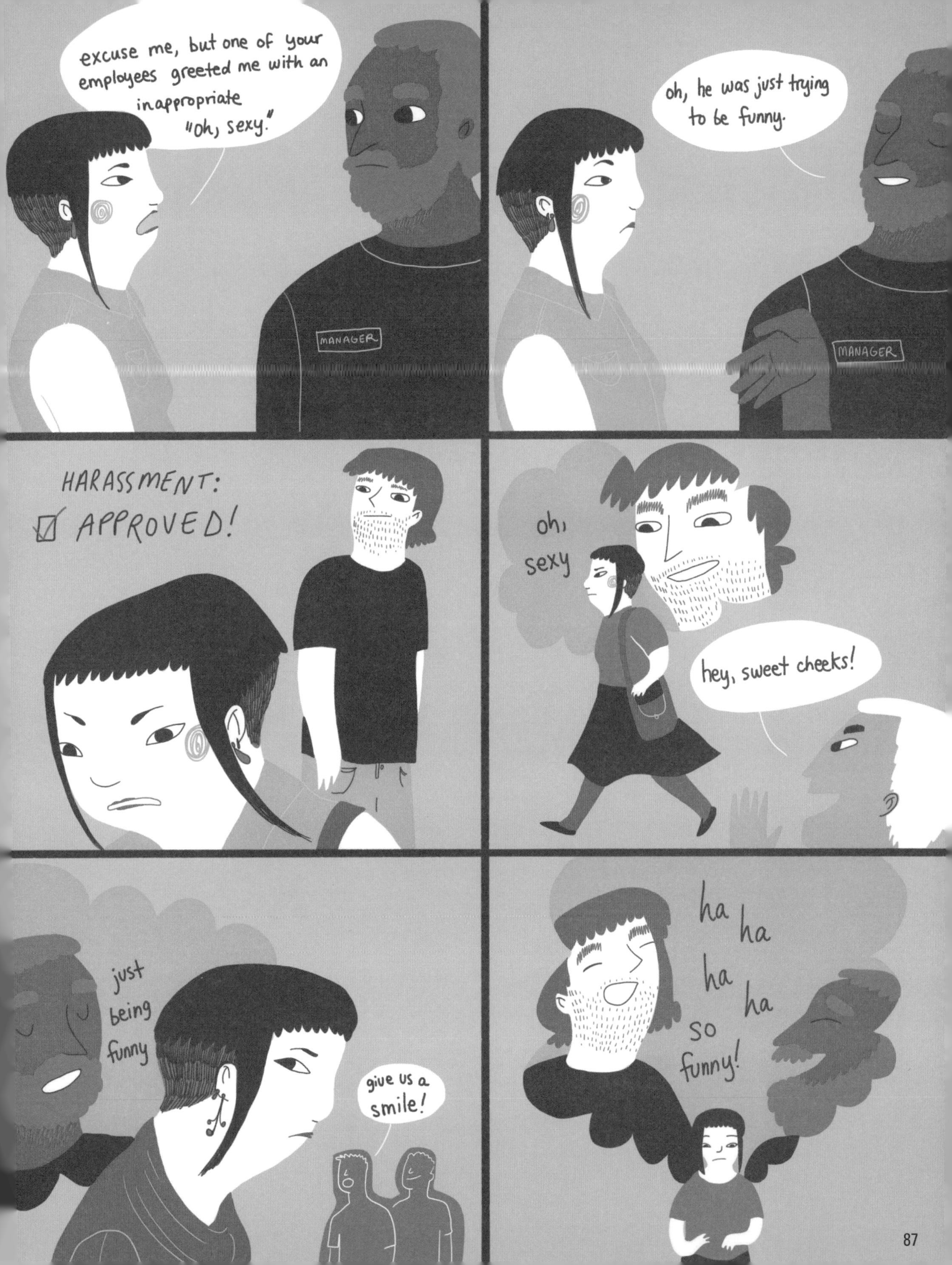
excuse me, but one of your employees greeted me with an inappropriate "oh, sexy."
oh, he was just trying to be funny.
MANAGER
MANAGER
HARASSMENT: APPROVED!
oh, sexy
hey, sweet cheeks!
just being funny
give us a smile!
ha ha ha ha so funny!

TWENTY

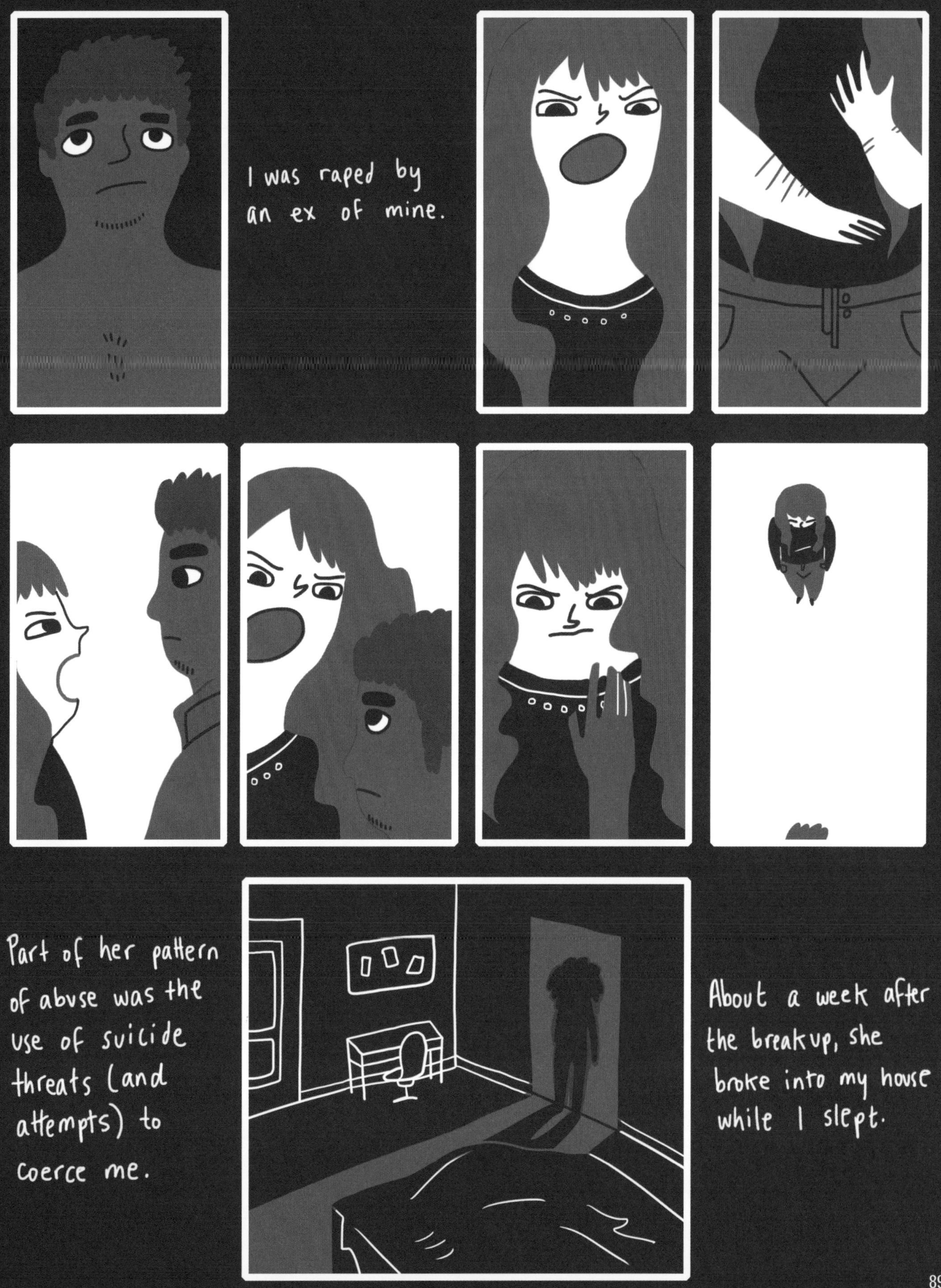

I was raped by an ex of mine.
Part of her pattern of abuse was the use of suicide threats (and attempts) to coerce me.
About a week after the breakup, she broke into my house while I slept.

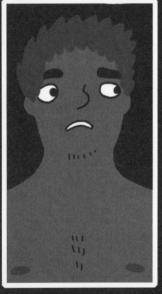

I had no idea
what to do

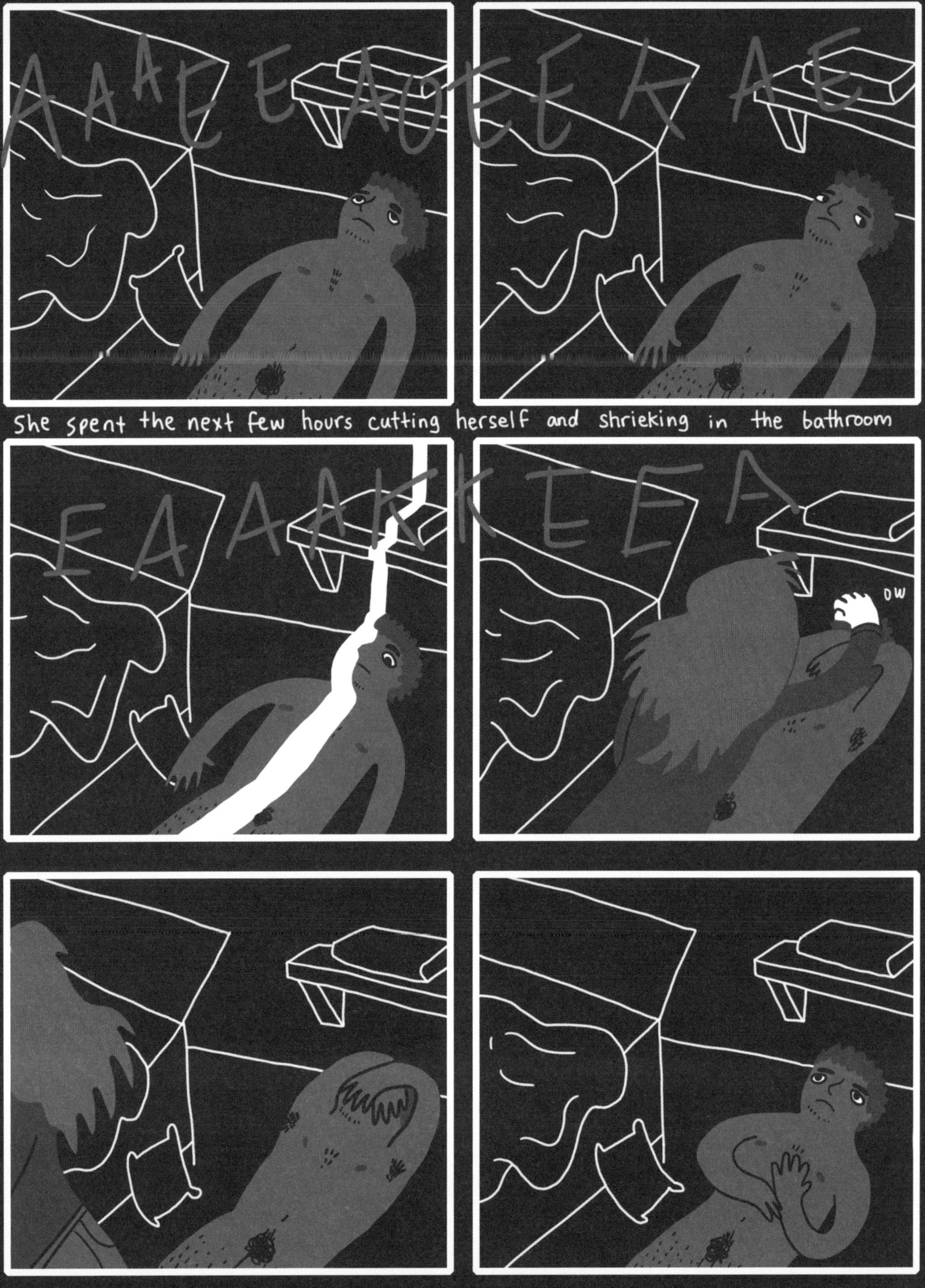
AAAEEAOEEEKAE
She spent the next few hours cutting herself and shrieking in the bathroom
EAAKEEA
OW

I changed my locks, but I kept finding written messages from her.

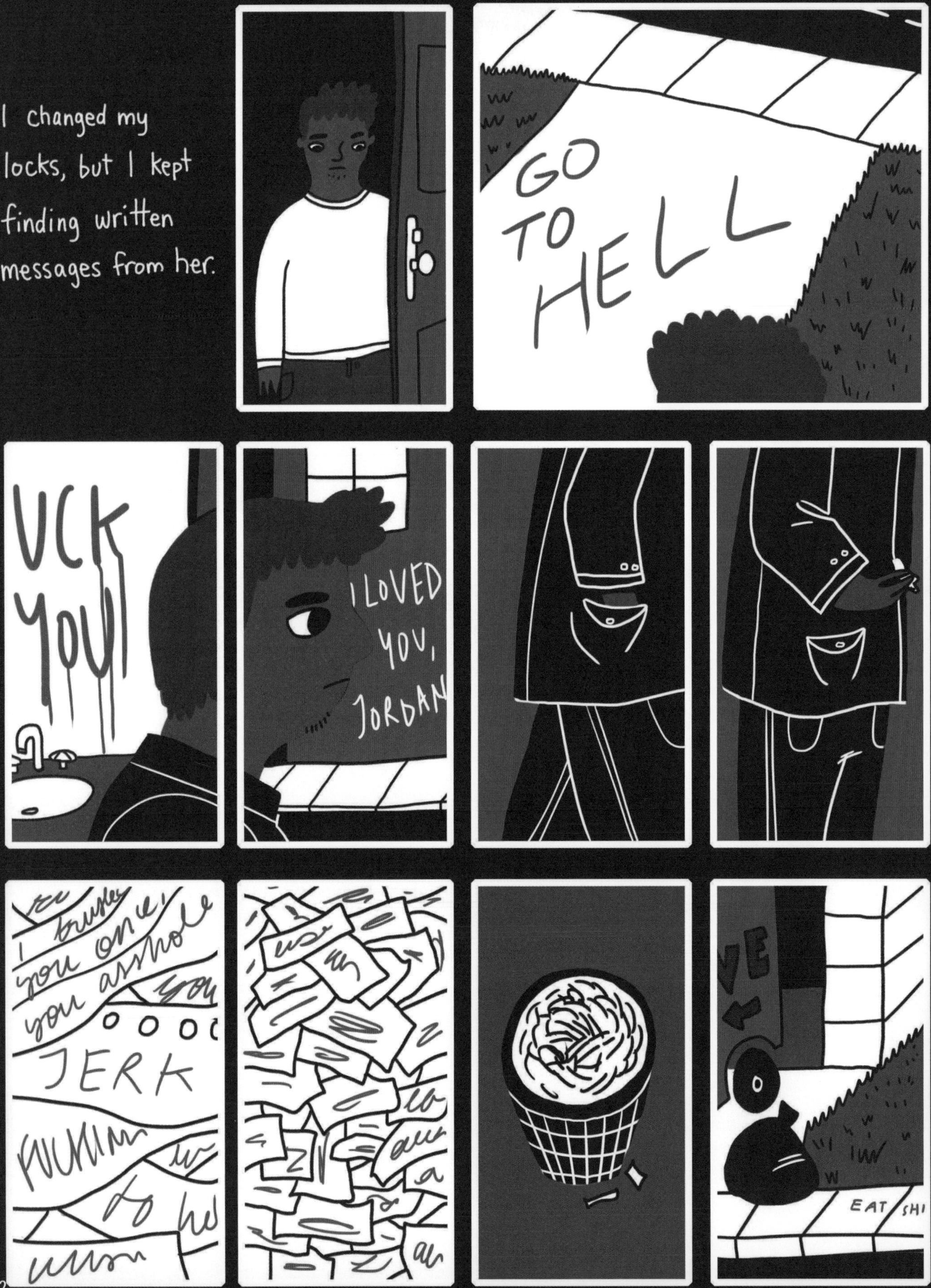
GO TO HELL
UCK YOU
I LOVED YOU, JORDAN
I trusted you once
you asshole
JERK
EAT SHI

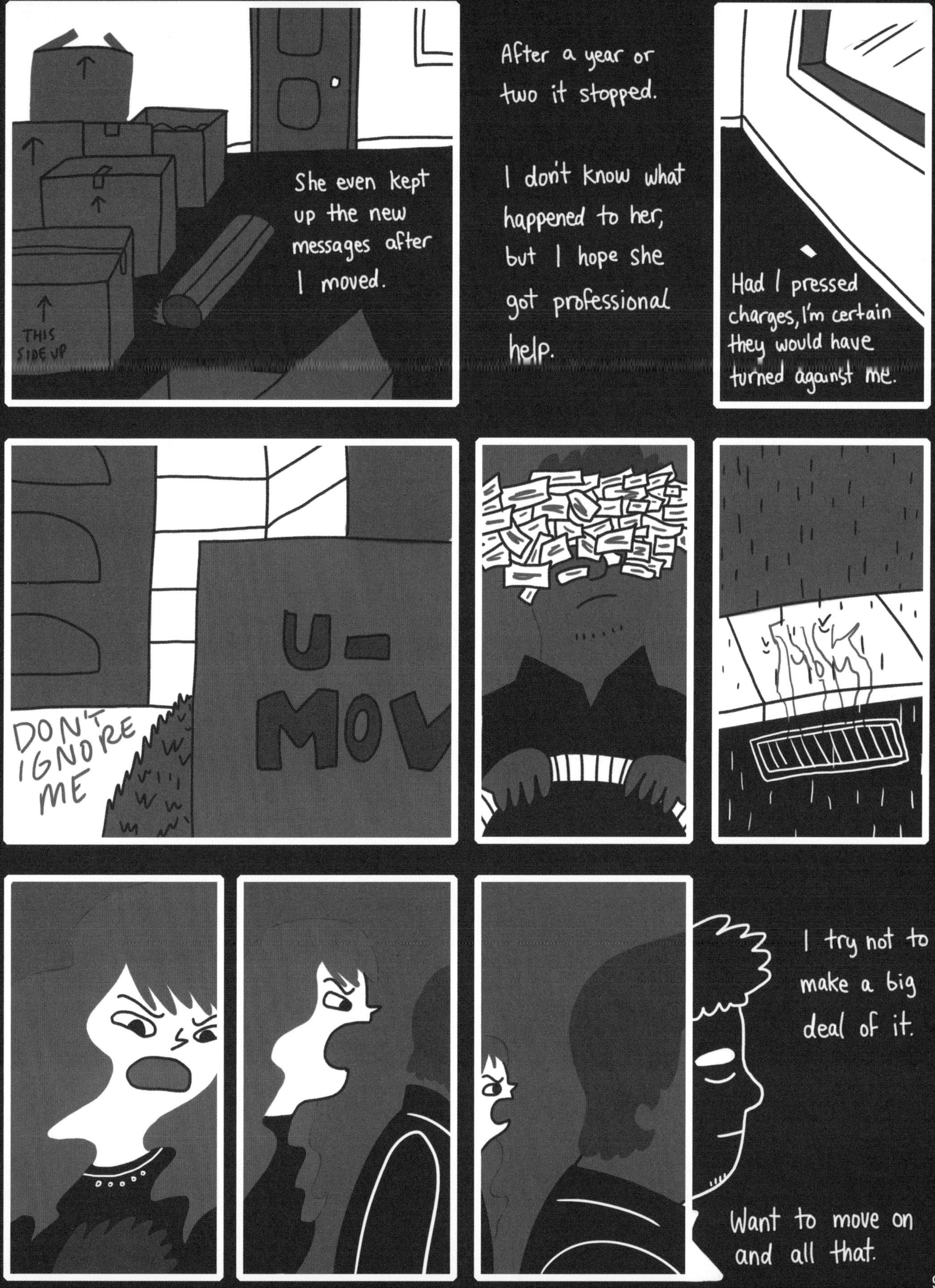
She even kept up the new messages after I moved.
THIS SIDE UP
After a year or two it stopped.
I don't know what happened to her, but I hope she got professional help.
Had I pressed charges, I'm certain they would have turned against me.
DON'T IGNORE ME
U-MOV
I try not to make a big deal of it.
Want to move on and all that.

NOTES

The stories in this book were mostly submitted online anonymously, some in the form of interviews. The process was a constant discussion and sharing of experiences, always a new "Hey, that happened to me too." It is both distressing (that these stories are so common) and provides hope that in sharing we can make it easier for survivors to deal with their experiences, and create a society that does not tolerate sexual violence.

LISTEN

Listen to what survivors have to say. It's often difficult to discuss, so be patient and be attentive. Do not be dismissive of their experiences. Survivors' stories are too often unheard and unbelieved, and this keeps people from speaking out. Survivors can feel safe to talk about their experiences, whether they are seeking comfort or justice, and this starts with one pair of ears at a time.

SUPPORT

Be supportive of survivors, in whatever way suits them best. It could involve talking about the issue, or it could be that they aren't ready. Be sensitive about anything that might trigger their experiences. This applies to personal relationships to individuals, or to people in general, especially online. Ask questions about how you can help.

WATCH

Be aware of the signs of uncomfortable or potentially dangerous situations. The overly jealous partner who is isolating their partner. A stranger talking to a young girl who clearly isn't interested. Watch for situations where someone isn't taking "no"—implied or direct—for an answer.

STOP

Intervene when you see it's necessary. When we stay silent when others are hurt, we are telling attackers that their actions are valid. This of course applies to dangerous situations, but also to the small things. Often a person knows their attacker. They might both be your friends. When a friend says something sexist, or jokes about sexual assault, interrupt. Have a discussion.

REACH OUT

As a survivor, you deserve to find your peace. Don't be afraid to let yourself find support—there are networks out there for you. Helplines and rape crisis centres are staffed by trained professionals who understand what you are going through. Even if you aren't ready to talk about it, there are people out there—close friends, counsellors, friends you haven't met yet— who can support you in the ways that suit you best.

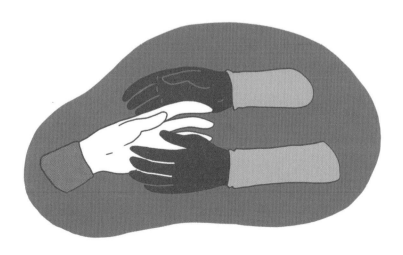

THANK YOU